Historical Staffordshire

American Patriots & Views

Jeffrey B. Snyder

with
Price
Guide

Schiffer
Publishing Ltd

77 Lower Valley Road, Atglen, PA 19310

Dedication

To my parents, James J. and Mary Alice Snyder, who
sparked my interest in history, archaeology and literature
early in my life.

Copyright © 1995 by Schiffer Publishing Ltd.
Library of Congress Cataloging-in-Publication Data

Snyder, Jeffrey B.
   Historical Staffordshire: American patriots and views:
   with price guide/ Jeffrey B. Snyder
p.   cm.
   Includes bibliographical references (p.   ) and Index.
   IBSN 0-88740-721-8
   1. Staffordshire pottery--Collectors and collecting--Catalogs.
2. Pottery--19th century--England--Staffordshire--Collectors
and collecting--Catalogs. 3. United States--History--Pictorial
works--Catalogs. 4. United States in art--Catalogs. I. Title.
NK4087.S6S56 1994
738.3'09424'6075--dc20   94-37617 CIP

Printed in Hong Kong

We are interested in hearing from authors
with book ideas on related topics.

Book Design By Balbach

Published by Schiffer Publishing Ltd.
77 Lower Valley Road
Atglen, PA 19310
Please write for a free catalog.
This book may be purchased from the publisher.
Please include $2.95 postage.
Try your bookstore first.

Contents

Acknowledgments

I wish to express my gratitude to the people who made this book possible. Dealers and collectors generously allowed me into their shops and homes, permitting me to disrupt their schedules and clutter their working and living spaces with a tangle of equipment. They made the photographs in this book possible. I offer my thanks to: William R. & Teresa F. Kurau–(dealers with printed catalogues), P.O. Box 457, Lampeter, PA 17537, (717) 464-0731–and Lynn D. Trusdell.

Introduction

The American Revolutionary War and the War of 1812 were times of trials, deprivation and separation for the citizenry of the developing United States of America. Battles tore through town and countryside, the new capitol city burned and harbors were choked with British embargoes. Ill-recorded in the histories of those trying times was the common grumble from citizenry and merchant alike, "When will these cursed wars end so I can get my hands on that English Staffordshire pottery again?"

Battles tore through American towns and countryside alike. Depicted here is the first great battle of the American Revolution, the Battle of Bunker Hill, Boston, Massachusetts. In June, 1775, British troops forced American soldiers from their fort on Breed's Hill to Bunker Hill. However, the Americans retreated only after they ran out of ammunition and not before many British soldiers had fallen. The battle proved that American forces could inflict heavy losses on the British army. As a result, the colonies were encouraged to send both men and supplies into the war. **The Battle of Bunker Hill**, enclosed with a vine border, transfer printed on a vegetable bowl by Ralph Stevenson. *Courtesy of the Collection of William R. & Teresa F. Kurau.*

Prior to the Revolution, earthenwares and stonewares produced in England were of comparable quality and better priced than most of what was offered from Europe. Well aware of this fact, American consumers and merchants alike chaffed under the temporary shortages in wares from the Staffordshire potting district of England imposed by war. Enterprising British merchants, disinclined to entangle profits with patriotism, slipped what shipments they could through by way of neutral Dutch merchants. British military officers also provided a tiny trickle of goods to the black market. American potters struggled to provide wares to fill the void; however, their British counterparts had convinced the now-revolutionary colonists so well of their wares' quality that America's native potters could make no real inroads into the American market.[1]

Still, while both wars finished in America's favor, much blood had been spilled, mayhem caused, ill-will generated, and restrictive English trade embargoes lifted. To thwart the threat of the loss of a lucrative market as one of the hazards of war, the potters of Staffordshire in 1815 turned to anti-government tactics they had used successfully to bolster sales before. They began decorating their wares with transfer printed pro-American patriotic scenes and visages. Running short on those, the potters turned to American scenic views which had begun to appear in books. Historical Staffordshire was the success the potters hoped for, an economic victory where the military had failed.

The British potters of Staffordshire decorated their wares with transfer printed pro-American patriotic scenes and personages in an attempt to offset the ill-will generated among Americans by the War of 1812. One such scene was **Commodore MacDonnough's Victory** shown here on a 10" plate produced by Enoch Wood & Sons. *Courtesy of the Collection of William R. & Teresa F. Kurau.*

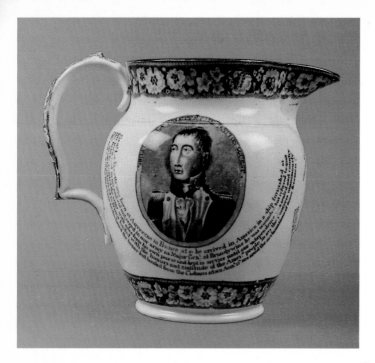

The Marquis de Lafayette was one of the figures of the American Revolution frequently found on historical Staffordshire wares. Immensely popular, the French general who fought along side his friend George Washington, returned to America in 1824. Lafayette's return led to many printed images commemorating the event including this **General Lafayette ... Welcome to the Land of Liberty** pitcher, by Andrew Stevenson. The pitcher measures 7 3/4" high. *Courtesy of the Collection of William R. & Teresa F. Kurau.*

Plucking the patriotic heartstrings of the new nation were the pottery works run by the Adams and Clews families, by Stevenson, Stubbs, Wood and many others. Historical Staffordshire wares were popular, durable, mass-produced in quantity and reasonably priced. They reached a wide audience. Their efforts have left us with fascinating glimpses of the American past, of images which once fired the passions and imaginations of the citizenry of a new nation.

Historical Staffordshire wares decorated with American patriots, British military defeats and scenic views were among the first of many decorated nineteenth century wares British potteries would produce specifically for the American market. These wares were decorated with transfer prints applied first to pearlware and later to a number of durable white wares. The earliest of these transfer printed images offered political or patriotic images in a deep cobalt blue popular in the United States. These were followed in the 1820s and 1830s by American views and a wider range of colors. Such prints included individual buildings, towns, idyllic landscapes, and modes of transportation. They were most frequently placed on plates and serving dishes, although mugs, pitchers, foot baths, and chamber pots also saw their share.

Running short of patriotic personalities and scenes, potters turned to American scenic views including this **Belleville On The Passaic River** view on the side of the soup tureen. The view of the **Hope Mill, Catskill, State of New York** is printed on the undertray. The lid features **New York Bay.** This very rare tureen was produced by Ralph Stevenson and measures 7 3/4" high, 11" x 8 1/2". *Courtesy of the Collection of William R. & Teresa F. Kurau.*

This pleasant view, **New York From Heights Near Brooklyn**, was originally created by the Irish artist W. G. Wall during his 1818 tour of America. The work appeared in Wall's book *Hudson River Port Folio*. Wall was given credit for his work on the printed back mark when the work was reproduced by Andrew Stevenson. Stevenson applied this print to a variety of wares including this large platter. *Courtesy of the Collection of William R. & Teresa F. Kurau.*

In the 1820s views of individual buildings began to appear including **Mitchell & Freemans China and Glass Warehouse, Chatham Street, Boston**. This plate was potted by William Adams and Son, measuring 10 1/4" in diameter. *Courtesy of the Collection of William R. & Teresa F. Kurau.*

Above right, right: Innovations in transportation were also printed on historical Staffordshire wares. The **Entrance of the Erie Canal Into The Hudson** and **Fulton Steam Boat** (so called) are two examples. The Erie Canal print was produced by Enoch Wood and Sons. This example appeared on a small plate measuring 6" in diameter. The Fulton Steam Boat was printed on a 10" plate by an unidentified manufacturer. The scene is not of any American port-of-call but was still popular in the United States. *Courtesy of the Collection of William R. & Teresa F. Kurau.*

The Staffordshire potting district of England was a major center of British ceramics manufacturing. By the middle of the nineteenth century two-thirds of England's potting industry, a total of 133 factories, would call Staffordshire home. The district encompassed the towns of Burslem, Cobridge, Dresden, Etruria, Fenton, Longport, Longton, Hanley, Shelton, Stoke-on-Trent, and Tunstall. Stoke-on-Trent provided Staffordshire with a rail hub.[2]

The wares we will concern ourselves with here were produced for the American market from within a few years of the signing of the Treaty of Ghent on December 24, 1814, officially ending the War of 1812, to roughly 1860. Historical Staffordshire was at it's height of popularity between roughly 1820 and 1845. More recent wares, post-1880, were produced by Minton and Company, Rowland and Marsellus Company, and Wedgwood and are beyond the scope of this work.

Chapter One

Origins

Historical Staffordshire wares were, in part, an end-product of English potters' quest for an inexpensive earthenware body which could compete with Chinese export porcelains. During the period from the late 1770s through the early 1800s, British potters would achieve this goal, developing several earthenware bodies presenting a surface white enough to rival the Chinese porcelains. They were also durable enough to survive rough trans-oceanic voyages to foreign markets.

The designs on historical Staffordshire wares were examples of an early mass production technique of the growing Industrial Revolution, transfer printing. England's potters developed the technique during the eighteenth century and perfected it in the nineteenth. Industrialization was providing British potters with the most rapidly growing stock of earthenware bodies in history; transfer printing allowed them to quickly produce large numbers of identically decorated wares from this stock for the first time in potting history. Together the new, white earthenware bodies and the transfer printed patterns would provide a popular, quality ware at a fairly low price, a ware many families of modest means could afford in America.

This combination of a durable, quality ware and mass produced decoration would also help propel Britain into dominance of the international ceramics marketplace and historical Staffordshire wares into growing popularity in America.

Earthenwares

Earthenwares are ceramic wares with soft, water-absorbent bodies made impermeable by glazing. These wares have been produced for centuries in England and elsewhere. Glazes consisting of lead sulfides with additives introduced to add color or opacity to an otherwise colorless and transparent substance were applied over these bodies, rendering them non-porous and resistant to chippage. Earthenwares, as opposed to higher fired stonewares and porcelain, were the predominant body types to which historical Staffordshire decorations were applied.[1]

Creamware and Pearlware

During the second half of the eighteenth century, English potters, particularly those of the Staffordshire district, refined their earthenwares. The bodies became thinner and harder. The body color was lightened to nearly that of the coveted Chinese porcelain's white. After 1750 these improvements led to creamware, a thin, hard-fired, cream colored earthenware dipped in a clear glaze. Josiah Wedgwood

may have perfected creamware, or Queen's ware, in 1762. From 1765 to the early 1770s Josiah Wedgwood experimented with the potting of a ware whiter than creamware which he christened "Pearl White" (pearlware) in 1779. By increasing the flint content in the body of the ware itself and adding a small quantity of cobalt to the glaze to offset the bodies natural yellow tint, Wedgwood presented a ware with a very white surface. One way to recognize pearlware is by the blue coloration of the glaze where it pools in crevices in the wares and a blue tint overall to the glaze itself.[2]

In the quest for an English refined earthenware which could compete with the popular Chinese export porcelain, creamware was the first successful result. It had a thin, hard-fired, cream colored body which was decorated, at times, with early transfer prints. **George Washington, Esq. General & Commander in Chief of the Continental Army in America** was printed on a creamware mug measuring 5 1/8" high. The manufacturer is unidentified. *Courtesy of the Collection of William R. & Teresa F. Kurau.*

By 1787 there were at least eight factories known to have been producing pearlware under the guise of "china glaze, blue painted" in Burslem alone. One of the factories also proclaimed itself an "enameller and printer of cream colour and china glaze ware." This is significant as it shows that transfer printing on pearlware had begun by 1787.

Pearlware gradually overtook creamware in popularity as the tableware of choice. By the early 1800s pearlware had so completely surpassed creamware as to reduce the latter to the cheapest tableware on the market. Pearlware came to be used for everything from dining services to chamber pots; however, it appeared most frequently in the form of shell-edged plates with rims painted either blue or green. Early historical Staffordshire wares were produced on pearlware.[3]

By the early 1800s, pearlware had completely surpassed creamware as the tableware of choice. Pearlware appeared most frequently in the form of shell-edged plates with rims painted either blue or green. Early historical Staffordshire prints were produced on pearlware as seen here in these examples by James & Ralph Clews. The prints are of General Lafayette and are entitled **Welcome Lafayette The Nation's Guest And Our Country's Glory**. Blue and green feather edged examples such as the small, central platter were very popular in early nineteenth century households. However, in the early years of the nineteenth century Elizabeth Lee -- the wife of the retired Congressman Richard Bland Lee -- wrote from her Virginia home, Sully plantation, to her sister in Philadelphia. Elizabeth Lee, who strove to keep her home decorated in the best Philadelphia fashion, complained that she would have to replace all of her feather edged pearlware as it was often found broken. She believed the household slaves considered pearlware decorated this way to be cheap and mishandled it. Popular though it was, pearlware could not please everyone. Left to right: cup plate -- 4 5/8" in diameter, small platter -- 10 1/2" x 8", small plate -- 6 3/4" in diameter. *Courtesy of the Collection of William R. & Teresa F. Kurau.*

As an interesting aside, archaeological excavations and historical documentation have thrown into doubt both the 1779 date for pearlware's introduction and the credit commonly given to Josiah Wedgwood for it's development. Three North American archaeological sites dating from August of 1778 to August of 1779 and Wedgwood's own correspondence contain the evidence.

The North American archaeological evidence dating from the years of the Revolutionary War is particularly startling as the common belief was that English trade restrictions effectively kept English product from rebel shores until after 1783. An added twist is that two of the three sites are American military sites (hardly where you would expect to find English wares during the Revolution): a sunken privateer Defence, lost on the Maine coast in August of 1779 while Wedgwood was still contemplating a name for his new white-bodied ware, and an American artillery camp in Pluckemin, New Jersey which was in operation only from December of 1778 to June of 1779. The third site was the wreck of the HMS Orpheus, scuttled in Narragansett Bay in August of 1778. A form of pearlware was recovered from all three sites, each well pre-dating Wedgwood's introduction of his "pearl white" ware.[4]

Josiah Wedgwood's correspondence during the 1770s also suggests the existence of some ware similar to his pearl white ware prior to it's introduction. In several letters he mentions four different names for wares which scholars now consider to be one-in-the-same, pearlware. These names were "blue and white", "china glaze", "white wares" and finally Wedgwood's own "pearl white." In a letter dated March 8, 1779, Wedgwood wrote to his partner Bentley asking his opinion on a name for his new ware. Wedgwood wrote "...to give the brat a name you may set a cream-colour plate and one of the best blue and white ones before you, and suppose the one you are to name another degree whiter and finer still." This letter refers to three wares, Wedgwood's old creamware, his new white ware (to be named Pearl White), and a blue and white ware which was already being produced by others.

Both written and physical evidence indicate that pearlware was available prior to Wedgwood's pearl white ware. The explanation for Josiah Wedgwood receiving credit for the feat, although apparently not from his contemporaries, had more to do with clever marketing than true innovation. The other manufacturers, unnamed and overlooked, failed to differentiate their white ware in any way from Wedgwood's creamware. Wedgwood, however, by naming his product pearl white in 1779 set it apart qualitatively from the rest. The implication was that his was both different and better than the rest.[5]

This new evidence suggests that pearlware in some form existed in 1778 and possibly as early as 1775. Historical Staffordshire wares decorated with American patriots and views first appeared on pearlware after c. 1815, well after it's inception, whenever that may have been. Shortly thereafter, in the 1820s, more durable white bodied earthenwares replaced pearlware as the body of choice to carry these images.

White Wares, Semi-Porcelains and Ironstones

In the 1820s pearlware would be replaced by more durable white wares and semi-porcelains which evolved out of it. White wares had a harder and whiter paste than pearlware and a clearer colorless glaze unavailable in pearlware. These ran parallel to the "stone china" produced by Spode in 1805 and Charles James Mason's famous "Ironstone China" patented in the Staffordshire Potteries in July of 1813. "Mason's Patent Ironstone China" was the best attempt to perfect a new and inexpensive but durable earthenware body during the early nineteenth century. The name alone conveyed a sense of strength associated in the public mind with china. Mason's Ironstone was an improvement on white ware with a harder body and a thinner and finer profile than other wares called ironstone. As with pearlware before it, small amount of cobalt blue was introduced into the glaze to make ironstone appear whiter than it would if its body paste were left exposed beneath a clear glaze. This process often left a pale blue puddling in crevices around handles and along the interior edges of foot rings while overall the glaze remained clear.[6]

The most accurate way of identifying these wares is from the manufacturer's mark which appears on the back of flat wares and on the bottom of hollow forms of most, beginning in the early nineteenth century. However, ironstone has been called many things by various manufacturers in an attempt to lure prospective consumers to their particular ware by making it seem special or unique ... the way Josiah Wedgwood did with pearlware. Some of the creative names applied to ironstone include "Granite China," "Opaque China," "Stone China," and "Stone ware."[8]

The most accurate form of identification for the body type of the popular white wares is provided by the manufacturers' marks where they are named. However, ironstone was called many things by many manufacturers in an attempt to make their ware seem unique. In this Thomas Godwin manufacturer's mark, the term "Opaque China" was used. *Courtesy of the Collection of William R. & Teresa F. Kurau.*

Most historical Staffordshire designs were applied to one form of white-bodied ware or another, including this example of the **Marine Hospital, Louisville, Kentucky** by Enoch Wood & Sons. Wood & Sons christened their white wares "Semi China." This plate measures 9" in diameter. *Courtesy of the Collection of William R. & Teresa F. Kurau.*

Most historical Staffordshire designs were applied to one form of white-bodied ware or another, be it semi-porcelains or ironstones. While the early potting and decorative standards were not perfect, the unusual new wares were able to compete well with more expensive porcelains. So successful was Mason's Patent Ironstone China alone that practically every potter of the period from 1830 through 1880 made versions of it.[7]

Until the late 1840s white-bodied earthenwares were usually decorated with transfer prints or with painted shell-edged rims. During the 1850s plain, undecorated white wares became popular and in the decades after the Civil War undecorated wares were widely produced in both England and the United States. Considering this trend it is not surprising that the popularity of historical Staffordshire prints ebbs after 1860.[9]

At their best Mason's Ironstone and white wares closely rivaled porcelain. However, for everyday use they had the upper hand, used for everything from table and tea services to toilet wares during the nineteenth century. For historical Staffordshire they were certainly the enduring wares of choice.

Origins and Development of Transfer Printing

Complementing the development of durable and popular white-bodied ceramic wares was the creation of the first mass-produced decorations for ceramics, the transfer prints. Transfer printing allowed a potter to quickly duplicate a pattern by transferring it from a copper plate to a ceramic vessels via a specially treated paper. Transfer printing was much quicker and cheaper than the hand painting techniques used prior to its introduction. The process also allowed for the purchase of complete sets of dishes that were virtually identical, a feat never before possible with the hand painted wares.

Underglaze printing was first used about 1760 on English porcelain, which was over twenty years before its introduction on Staffordshire earthenwares. Underglaze blue printing on earthenwares was introduced around 1783 in Staffordshire.[11]

Once transfer printing was accepted by potters as a decorative technique, it quickly gained popularity with the public. The earliest patterns were Chinese designs which remained popular until roughly the War of 1812. The earliest transfer printed "chinoiseries," including the "willow pattern" were printed on pearlware.

Hand painted wares were largely replaced by the more quickly and cheaply produced transfer prints. Transfer prints could also be produced in nearly identical complete dinner sets. This was impossible with the painted wares. An extremely rare and beautiful example of hand painting is presented in this **View from Hyde Park, Hudson River** tray by Copeland & Garrett measuring 10 1/2" X 7 1/4". *Courtesy of the Collection of William R. & Teresa F. Kurau.*

Copeland & Garrett, Spode Works, Stoke, Staffordshire, 1833-1847, printed manufacturer's mark. This particular mark is reported to date from 1846. The name of the view is printed beneath the mark. *Courtesy of the Collection of William R. & Teresa F. Kurau.*

While Messrs. Janssen, Delamain and Brooks, at York House, Battersea, probably produced the earliest transfer prints in red and purple on white salt-glazed plates around 1753, Messrs. Sadler and Green of Liverpool are recognized for perfecting the technique in 1756. Sadler and Green produced black prints on delftware, a very soft bodied ware, and creamware. The early transfer prints were applied over top of the glaze. The "overglazed" patterns quickly showed signs of wear when used and were only truly suitable for decorative, not useful, pieces. Printing in underglaze blue on earthenwares would not become common until the end of the eighteenth century.[10]

Early in the nineteenth century some potters broke from the near obsession for copying Chinese designs colored in a deep cobalt blue. Cobalt blue was discovered to be the only color early on that would survive the high firing temperatures necessary for underglazing the design. Completely new designs came into fashion. Around 1802 wide borders, normally floral, became popular. Various potteries developed characteristic border designs which were rarely copied. These characteristic borders provide a useful means to identify a particular manufacturer when a manufacturers' mark is not present. They are far more reliable than the central pattern. Those patterns were frequently copied as there was no copyright law to protect them.[12]

Print quality improved during the early nineteenth century as engravers learned to use dots instead of lines to create their patterns through stippling. The dots acted as a shading device which provided greater perspective to the prints. The earliest dated ware with stippled engraving is from 1807.[13]

Early black transfer printed plaque by John Sadler dating from c. 1760. This plaque reflects the high quality of the early overglazed transfer printing technique Messrs. Sadler and Green are credited with perfecting in 1756. This plaque reads: The Right Honorable Wm. Pitt Esqr. One of His Majesty's Principal Secretaries of State and One of His Most Honorable Privy Council. J. Sadler, Liverpool. Mid-1700s. Josiah Wedgwood would soon provide much less flattering images of Mr. Pitt in unlikely wares. *Courtesy of the Collection of William R. & Teresa F. Kurau.*

The Staffordshire potters, beginning in c. 1802, developed wide decorative borders to surround their central transfer printed images. Most potteries designed specific borders they could call their own. Remarkably, unlike the central prints, these were rarely copied by other potters. Joseph Stubbs produced this "Spread Eagle" border. The center scene is of the **Park Theater, New York**, printed on a small plate measuring 6" in diameter. *Courtesy of the Collection of William R. & Teresa F. Kurau.*

Print quality improved as engravers learned to use dots instead of lines to create their patterns through stippling. The dots acted as a shading device, providing greater perspective to the prints. Stippling also allowed for the appearance of clouds. This idyllic scene is **Fair Mount Near Philadelphia** by Joseph Stubbs. It is printed on a 10 1/4" diameter plate. *Courtesy of the Collection of William R. & Teresa F. Kurau.*

The overall quality of the art work varied according to both the resources of the potter and his customers. The leading firms produced beautiful ceramics with finely engraved transfer printed patterns. Lesser firms produced simpler designs, frequently following the lead of their larger competitors.

Origins of Historical Staffordshire

English potters printing portraitures of American rebels and images of English defeats to promote American sales was not new idea to Staffordshire following the War of 1812. As Ivor Noël Hume aptly stated, "...to put pots before principle..." was an old habit in Staffordshire. During the War of 1812 industrious British engravers espoused the cause of American freedom with near-treasonable anti-government images of cringing British lions emblazoned with insulting slogans. These could be slipped out through the neutral Dutch and taken to shore by any number of unrecorded vessels navigating up lesser traveled American waterway. These ships avoided major ports of call such as Philadelphia where their scandalous wares would be discovered and confiscated before sale.[14]

In the eighteenth century Josiah Wedgwood lampooned leading members of the British government to promote English sales. On one occasion he placed the visage of a member of parliament, William Pitt, in the bottoms of "spitting pots and other vile utensils." This drew the poetical wrath of the future Lord High Chancellor of Great Britain, Lord Thurlow:

> "Lo! Wedgwood, too, waves his Pitt-pots on high!
> Lo! the points where the bottoms, yet dry,
> The visage immaculate bear!
> Be Wedgwood d----d and double d----d his ware."[15]

Around 1810, more innocent prints of English and foreign landscapes began to appear frequently on Staffordshire wares as well. The American scenes found within this book followed after the War of 1812 as many manufacturers further catered to American markets with the engraving of domestic and exotic foreign views or the arms of American states. These patterns, although remaining popular until approximately 1860, began to be replaced in the 1830s by romantic views.[16]

Of course not all of the printed wares for the home market produced in Staffordshire contained political barbs. The potters plucked native nationalistic heart-strings just as effectively as they did those in the American market. Two examples to prove the point: a 7" high pitcher entitled **Nelson, England Expects Every Man To Do His Duty** was produced by an unidentified manufacturer to commemorate the hero of the English Navy; another anonymous potter produced this 10 1/4" diameter plate holding high the memory of the late king George III entitled **Sacred to the Memory of George 3rd Who Died 29, January 1820**. *Courtesy of the Collection of William R. & Teresa F. Kurau.*

Following the War of 1812, Staffordshire's potters catered to the American markets with engravings of domestic and foreign views or the arms of American states. A series entitled Arms of the American States was produced by Thomas Mayer between 1826 and 1838 and included the seals of the original states, excluding New Hampshire. Here on a 20 3/4" x 15 3/4" platter is **Pennsylvania** and on a 12" x 10" x 4 1/4" fruit compote is **Virginia**. *Courtesy of the Collection of William R. & Teresa F. Kurau.*

By 1815 Great Britain has extricated itself from wars in North America and in Europe and begun to reap the harvest of the Industrial Revolution. Colonial and manufacturing empires maintained by the island nation and protected by the Royal Navy brought England into a position of world dominance in commerce, finance and transportation. Railways, import tariffs and the British Reform Movement were strengthening the nation from within as well. By the time Queen Victoria was crowned sovereign in 1837, a sense of security would permeate the nation.[1]

Prior to the American Revolution, creamware launched English potter's conquest of the world tableware market. So successful were the English potters that American colonial governments instituted aggressive "Buy American" plans, but to no avail. Efforts by domestic potters to compete with their English rivals were doomed to fail. The most notable attempt was the Bonnin and Morris porcelain factory in Philadelphia. This factory operated from 1770 to 1772. They produced tea wares with chinoiserie designs in blue underglaze to compete with porcelain from Bow, Derby and Lowestoft. The Philadelphia pottery failed in part due to technical and labor difficulties which kept costs uncompetatively high. The fact of the matter was, American works simply could not compete at that time with both the tidal wave of lower priced English wares and the firm belief that the imports were superior. With the exception of a few coarse red wares - the stuff of storage jugs and milk pans - English pottery dominated the American market.[2]

The English potters' success in producing a series of wares (pearlwares and a variety of white wares) white enough and hard enough to compete with Chinese export porcelain coupled with the growing quality and sophistication of their transfer printing techniques ensured them of preeminence in the American ceramics market until after the centennial of 1876. The bulk of these potters' wares were domestic tablewares, predominantly at low enough costs to attract many buyers.

Efforts by American potters to compete with their English rivals were doomed to fail. The most noteworthy attempt was that of the Bonnin and Morris porcelain factory in Philadelphia which produced porcelain tea wares from 1770 to 1772. The Pennsylvania Chronicle, January 15 - January 22, 1770, page 427, included an advertisement for Bonnin and Morris in the lower right hand corner of the page. Labor and technical difficulties combined with the firm American belief in the superiority of English wares led to the firms early demise. *Courtesy of the Collection of William R. & Teresa F. Kurau.*

To reestablish and assure this American preeminence in the early nineteenth century, once the inconveniences of the American Revolution and the War of 1812 were behind them, British potters manufactured wares calculated specifically to bolster their previously strong affiliations with American consumers. Despite the widespread destruction and hardship caused by the British military, the potting industry was able to salvage their relationship with American consumers through the judicious use of deep blue transfer prints featuring American patriotic themes, famous personages, and well-known scenic views. These wares were also priced well within the reach of an ever-increasing majority of Americans throughout the height of their popularity from 1820-1860.

American Cultural Change: Demand for New Wares Fire Historical Staffordshire's Popularity.

The positive effects of the Industrial Revolution which were improving production and distribution for English manufacturers were also at work in America. The new nation was rapidly changing from Thomas Jefferson's dream of an idyllic agrarian society into a boisterous industrial power certain of it's manifest destiny. America rapidly developed an escalating number of consumers in the market for a wide variety of manufactured wares.

The Changing American World

After the War of 1812, the young republic was a land transformed. The Louisiana Purchase, Thomas Jefferson's bargain buy from Napoleon, doubled the nation's size, adding the land from the Mississippi River to the Rocky Mountains. This was, of course, news to the Indian nations already established in this territory. The port of New Orleans was secured once-and-for-all by the end of the War of 1812. The American vision of the land itself was transformed. To the Puritans, wilderness had been considered a land of devils and demons, a domain to be feared. To early nineteenth century Americans, the land held beauties to be reveled in and rhapsodized about. More importantly, the newly acquired open spaces were viewed as opportunity for future fortunes to be won.[3]

Culturally the Industrial Revolution was transforming a nation as well. Largely a nation of farmers with few personal possessions in the eighteenth century, the nineteenth century populace was becoming a more urban population willing and able to gather in the growing harvest of goods provided by industrialization, including —- of course —- the pottery from Staffordshire.

Patriotism ran high. The years 1816 to 1824 would be dubbed the "Era of Good Feelings," a time marked by diminished political wrangling and heightened national pride. The events leading to nationhood had provided an established group of war heroes with tales of deeds of daring-do to tell, founding father's, and dignified statesmen on which to focus the national pride and patriotic fervor. These fig-

ures —- George Washington, Benjamin Franklin, Thomas Jefferson, General Lafayette and DeWitt Clinton among them —- provided the first opportunity for the Staffordshire potters to make amends and regain their American market. Some of the most popular of the historical Staffordshire wares produced in this period and for this purpose were those commemorating the emotionally charged return visit of General Lafayette to the United States in 1824. James and Ralph Clews of Cobridge, England captured Lafayette's landing at Castle Garden in the New York Battery on their wares. Enoch Wood, a determined competitor to the Clews, provided touching scenes of the General mourning at the tombs of his departed allies, Benjamin Franklin and George Washington. Wood went further, following that time-honored Staffordshire tradition of creating what would be considered a scandalous print at home of the brilliant defeat of a British squadron by American Commodore MacDonnough on Lake Champlain in 1814. The deep blue transfer print was surrounded by a striking shell border appropriate to the nautical theme and to a rising popular interest in the natural world.[4]

Printing flattering images of heroes of the American struggle for independence and of dignified American statesmen were among the Staffordshire potters first attempt to make amends and regain their American market. Ralph Stevenson and Williams, c. 1825, produced this four medallion portrait featuring Thomas Jefferson, George Washington, General Lafayette and DeWitt Clinton. The central view is of the **Park Theater, New York** with a small inset of an Erie canal print entitled **Entrance Of The Canal Into The Hudson At Albany**. The plate measures 10" in diameter. *Courtesy of the Collection of William R. & Teresa F. Kurau.*

Some of the most popular of the earlier historical Staffordshire wares commemorated the emotionally charged return visit of General Lafayette to American shores in 1824. James and Ralph Clews produced this image **Welcome Lafayette The Nation's Guest And Our Country's Glory** to mark the event. Accompanying this printed cup plate by the Clews brothers is a snuff box presented to Washington Lafayette McNair, the five year old son of Governor Alexander McNair (1775-1826) -- the first governor of Missouri -- by General Lafayette at a state dinner in St. Louis in 1824. Lafayette presented the snuff box as a token of appreciation for the gift the young McNair had presented him, a gold mounted cane from a branch of a tree near George Washington's tomb. The cup plate measures 4 5/8" in diameter. *Courtesy of the Collection of William R. & Teresa F. Kurau.*

The Clews brothers also produced **The Landing Of General Lafayette At Castle Garden, New York, 16 August, 1824** to commemorate the moment of Lafayette's arrival. Here the scene is printed on a covered vegetable dish measuring 9 1/2" x 6". *Courtesy of the Collection of William R. & Teresa F. Kurau.*

Above right, right: Enoch Wood & Sons (1818-1846), a determined competitor of Clews, provided heart-warming scenes of the General mourning at the tombs of his departed allies, Benjamin Franklin and George Washington. On the 5 1/4" high sugar bowl Lafayette reflects at Franklin's tomb, the image succinctly entitled **Lafayette At Franklin's Tomb. Lafayette at Washington's Tomb** adorns a 10" diameter plate. *Courtesy of the Collection of William R. & Teresa F. Kurau.*

Wood & Sons went further, creating a scandalous print by English standards of the brilliant defeat of a British naval squadron by Commodore MacDonnough on Lake Champlain in 1814. Titled **Commodore MacDonnough's Victory**, this image was printed on a 10" diameter plate. *Courtesy of the Collection of William R. & Teresa F. Kurau.*

The eastern third of the United States was considered "tamed" during the first half of the nineteenth century and Americans were venturing forth to explore the countryside they now considered romantic. Rustic hotels were built in favorite scenic spots, including Niagara Falls. If you could not get to the view, the view could come to you on Staffordshire wares. Here Wood and Sons presented the view **Table Rock, Niagara** on a 11 1/2" diameter bowl. *Courtesy of the Collection of William R. & Teresa F. Kurau.*

The Natural World

By the end of the War of 1812, the American frontier — and battles with Native Americans over territory — had been pushed westward. The threat of war with European powers along the borders of the United States had eased. Americans had "tamed" enough of the eastern third of the continent to begin to view the countryside surrounding their expanding cities and towns as "romantic." Long, rough-hewn hotels cropped up in favorite spots such as Niagara Falls, New York and Newport, Rhode Island to accommodate sightseers. Following this trend, transfer printed landscapes illustrating the popular, romantic ideal of nature were produced. These images were heavily influenced by the Romantic Movement of the first half of the nineteenth century.[5]

The Romantic Movement either looked longingly back to the pre-Industrial age or towards the wonders of nature and their meaning. On historical Staffordshire wares, three subjects were considered most attractive in these views: scenes from literature and mythology, subjects of common human experience, and nostalgic, exotic, sublime or historical subjects. All were designed to produce predictable, preconditioned responses in the viewer.

Nature's landscapes were imbued with moral as well as emotional impact. Groves of trees created no mere forests, they were God's first temples. The messages carried within the motifs were expected to be discernable by all. With such images printed on plates and platters, meals were to become both educational and uplifting affairs.[6]

Coupled with the views of the Romantic Movement, the improved transportation systems of the nineteenth century allowed Victorians all over the western world to explore the world. From this a passion for natural history developed. This passion had Victorians chronicling what they did not consume of the world's flora, fauna and sea life, creating museums for their discoveries, erecting home conservatories and publishing illustrated volumes on the natural sciences. Staffordshire artists were sent thumbing through botany texts, and visiting botanical gardens and zoos, sketch pads in hand, for inspiration. Some of this fascination may be seen in the border designs created by several of the potters of historical Staffordshire wares.[7]

Another reason for the popularity of a romantic image of wooded mountains, sandy shores, and even idyllically set American towns may be traced to the actual dirtiness and difficulty of life in both rural and urban landscapes. Farms were rugged places for all but the wealthiest gentlemen farmers as may be expected, but the growing cities were far worse. Cities were densely populated, poorly drained and rarely cleaned. Streets were covered in thick layers of horse manure. In some areas of town people swore they had not seen the actual road bed in living memory. Permeating the nostrils of every city dweller was the stench of the slaughterhouses and the tanneries. Almost every city also had herds of free-roaming pigs. Charles Dickens remarked of New York's pigs in the early 1840s, "Take care of the pigs. Two portly sows are trotting up behind this carriage, and a select party of half a dozen gentlemen hogs have just now turned the corner... They are the city scaven-

Chronicling the natural world became a nineteenth century fascination for Victorians steeped in the Romantic Movement and freed by new and varied forms of transportation. Many volumes on the natural sciences were produced filled with illustrations the Staffordshire potters found useful. Conchology was among the growing areas of study as is evident here in the shell and seaweed border created by Enoch Wood & Sons. The shell border with the irregular center surrounds the image which has come to be known as **Cadmus** after the ship that brought Lafayette to America in 1824. The plate measures 10" in diameter. *Courtesy of the Collection of William R. & Teresa F. Kurau.*

gers, these pigs." They were also a food source for the poor, although many people were sickened as a result. Pigs dining on city garbage make a poor food source.[8]

Historical Staffordshire scenes and landscapes, country and city views alike, were pristine by comparison. Several of the city views do show cattle and sheep in the foreground, but the cleanliness even of these scenes would provide at least temporary escape from the dirtiness of the real world. Gazing down into clean views of towns and countryside, urbanites and farmers alike could dream of roaming in fantasy lands free of mud, manure and stench.

Historical Staffordshire scenes and landscapes were pristine when compared to the dirtiness and difficulties of everyday life. Several of the city views do show cattle, sheep and horses in the foreground, but the cleanliness even of these scenes would provide at least temporary relief from the real world. Andrew Stevenson (1816-1830) produced a lovely vista, **New York from Weehawk**, based on the art work of W. G. Wall and Enoch Wood & Sons created an eye-pleasing view of **Castle Garden, Battery, New York**. Note there are no pigs, debris, or even crowds in sight in these pleasant views. The Stevenson view was printed on a platter measuring 18 1/2" x 14 1/4". The Wood & Sons view was placed on a large soup tureen measuring 10" high. *Courtesy of the Collection of William R. & Teresa F. Kurau.*

Developing Urban Life, Varying Aspects

From this fertile soil, American industry and opportunity bloomed. Factory towns rose quickly around waterfalls or river rapids, each supporting from two to ten mills, mansions for their owners and superintendents, and rows of houses for the mill hands. Families who once supported themselves on farms gradually gravitated to the cities and towns for industrial work. For many the agrarian life with all family members working together in the fields was left behind. Replacing this way of life was an urban world of work where fathers could support their families outside the home while women and children remained behind. Impressive manors and gothic cottages began to ring the larger cities as well, evidence of growing wealth with industrial innovation.[9]

Many of the transfer printed patterns on historical Staffordshire present tasteful views of urban structures and homes important in nineteenth century social and economic life. For example, the pottery manufacturers J. & W. Ridgway of Hanley, produced the Beauties of America series portraying public buildings from Massachusetts to Georgia engraved in great detail, including the Boston State House, Harvard University, Savannah Bank, The Capitol Building in Washington, D.C., and a variety of churches, halls and hospitals. Each plate was bordered with roses, adding natural beauty to the works of man. Fortunately for the collector, each scene was identified with a printed label on the back or bottom of each piece. This was the custom with many transfer printed wares, particularly those produced by large potting firms.

Charles Dickens toured American towns and countryside early in the 1840s, writing of his experiences and providing first hand, if somewhat biased, impressions of many of the structures illustrated in the Staffordshire prints.

Dickens wrote of the Boston State House, "In front is a green enclosure, called the Common. The site is beautiful: and from the top there is a charming panoramic view of the whole town and neighborhood." Of the business of state conducted within, he added, "Such proceedings as I saw here, were conducted with perfect gravity and decorum; and were certainly calculated to inspire attention and respect."

Moving south, at Philadelphia the abundance of water and the waterworks caught Dickens eye: "Philadelphia is most bountifully provided with fresh water, which is showered and jerked about, and turned on, and poured off everywhere. The Waterworks, which are on a height near the city, are no less ornamental than useful, being tastefully laid out as a public garden, and kept in the best and neatest order." His words sketch as pristine a picture of the works as does the transfer printed image.[10]

Job and John Jackson (1831-1835) produced one of several views of the Philadelphia water works. The abundance of water supplied to Philadelphia was a wonder to foreign travelers as indicated by the remark "Philadelphia is most bountifully provided with fresh water, which is showered and jerked about, and turned on, and poured off everywhere." This image, titled **The Water Works, Philadelphia**, was printed on a 9 1/8" diameter plate. *Courtesy of the Collection of William R. & Teresa F. Kurau.*

John and William Ridgway (1814-1830) produced the Beauties of America series portraying public buildings from Massachusetts to Georgia engraved in great detail. Their **State House, Boston** was printed here on a gravy boat measuring 3 1/2" high. *Courtesy of the Collection of William R. & Teresa F. Kurau.*

In Washington, D.C., Charles Dickens' lament is the same as that heard today from thousands of tourists lost in the nation's capitol annually, "Spacious avenues, that begin in nothing and lead nowhere..." The city was a work in progress far from completion, an aspect not projected in transfer printed images, "... streets, mile-long, that want only houses, roads and inhabitants; public buildings that need but a public to complete; and ornaments of great thoroughfares, which only lack great thoroughfares to ornament—are its leading features." Thinking little of the incompleteness of the young nation's capitol city, Dickens was even less impressed with the White House, "The President's mansion is more like an English clubhouse, ... "[11]

The President's House, Washington was not considered impressive by some English visitors who remarked that it had the appearance "... more like an English clubhouse ...". This image was produced by Job and John Jackson on a 10 3/8" diameter plate. *Courtesy of the Collection of William R. & Teresa F. Kurau.*

When John and William Ridgway produced this image of the **Capitol, Washington** when the nation's capitol building and city were unfinished works in progress. The final central dome familiar to viewers today would come later in the nineteenth century. This view of the Capitol was printed on a well and tree platter measuring 20 1/2" x 15 1/2". *Courtesy of the Collection of William R. & Teresa F. Kurau.*

Finally, back in Boston the inner workings of the Massachusetts Asylum for the Blind were described. Such government institutions were featured on several different historical Staffordshire pieces by competing potteries. About the location and workings of the asylum, Dickens wrote, "Like most other public institutions in America, of the same class, it stands a mile or two without the town, in a cheerful healthy spot...upon a height commanding the harbor...In a portion of the building, set apart for that purpose, are workshops for blind persons whose education is finished, and who have acquired a trade, but who cannot pursue it in the ordinary manufactory because of their deprivation." Those who have been educated but failed to work for their board were turned out, "Those who prove unable to earn their own livelihood will not be retained; as it is not desirable to convert the establishment into an almshouse, or to retain any but working bees in the hive."[12]

A variety of asylums were established at the edges of large towns and cities to take care of individuals with various handicaps. These were considered quite impressive and progressive by visitors and were portrayed as such in historical Staffordshire wares. **The Deaf & Dumb Asylum, Hartford Con.** was produced by J. & W. Ridgway on this 14 3/4" x 16 3/4" platter. *Courtesy of the Collection of William R. & Teresa F. Kurau.*

Of Churches and Museums, Congregants and Curiosities

John and William Ridgway also present several images of one of the more important social arenas of the early to mid-nineteenth century, the churches. Images of the Octagon and St. Paul's churches in Boston and Staughton's Church in Philadelphia are serene and dignified. Other potters would present equally inspirational views.

John and William Ridgway presented several images of one of the more important social arenas of the early to mid-nineteenth century, the churches. By mid-century the images produced by Staffordshire potters and the reality of the actual American churches would begin to merge. A beautiful view of the **Octagon Church, Boston** on a day when the Bostonian congregants were elsewhere. This was printed in the center of a fruit compote measuring 9 3/4" in diameter and 5 1/4" high. *Courtesy of the Collection of William R. & Teresa F. Kurau.*

For a growing number of Americans, worship services were becoming the most important social event of the week. Prior to the service, congregants clustered together outside to catch up on the news or to conduct a little business. The services themselves were long affairs, some with a second round in the afternoon.[13]

The early nineteenth century urban churches bore little resemblance to the peaceful and decorous settings on the British plates and platters. Many were cluttered with the remains of fruit and nuts brought in to sustain the congregants during the lengthy encounters with the word of God. Tobacco juice stained the floors and broken windows stuffed with old rags and hats were commonplace sights. Add to the scene family dogs frisking around the pews and the odd chicken or turkey in the summer and you have some feel for early nineteenth century worship.[14]

As the first quarter of the nineteenth century drew to a close, the Staffordshire image of American churches and reality began to merge. Dogs, turkeys and other fowl were banned. New standards of decorum were enforced. Windows were repaired and tobacco chewing and eating were slowly brought to a halt.[15]

One aspect of church life is noticeably absent from most historical Staffordshire prints, the church cemetery. This is no surprise as these were awful, overused and frequently abused sites of which no one wished to be reminded. With limited space, burials were frequently stacked one on top of another and the ground became a perpetual quagmire. At night these city sites were all too convenient for grave robbers and medical students. James Smillie wrote of the problem in 1847 "The impropriety of making interments beneath and around churches, and in the festering burial-grounds of cities, was generally acknowledged. Injurious to health, offensive to the senses, repulsive to the taste of a refined age, the practice had become a confessed nuisance, which all desired but none knew how to abate."[16]

However a rising fascination with nature and the Romantic Movement produced in the early nineteenth century both a solution to this urban problem and a movement which would have been totally foreign to the Founding Fathers of the eighteenth century. The Garden Cemetery Movement was born in Boston. Auburn Cemetery was created in 1832 as a result, a large rural cemetery in rolling countryside with plenty of room for adequate burials. The site was also far enough away from the city to make grave robbery prohibitively difficult. The garden cemetery landscape was adorned with sculptures and artful groupings of trees and flowers to combine a necessity for more burial land with a desire to revel in nature. Part of the impetus for this grew out of the notion that death itself could be romantic. The "deliverance from this mundane world, a glorious reunion with loved ones in the palace of heaven."[17]

The combination of sylvan burial plots and the notion of romantic death drove families out into the new, large, rural cemeteries on picnics. Young couples took long strolls and individuals wandered among sepulchers and statuary to seek out moral lessons and inspiration. In essence, the new cemeteries became the first American public parks.[18]

This combination of movements explains several unusual historical Staffordshire prints. Neither George Washington nor Benjamin Franklin would have ever expected anyone to spend time ruminating over their graves. Yet Enoch Wood & Sons in both **Franklin's Tomb** and **Washington's Tomb** depict General Lafayette reclining by urn capped tombs, following the new nineteenth century custom and drawing inspiration from the resting places of his departed allies. Edward and George Phillips (1822-1834) show a young couple gazing at a tomb in a open glade in their print **Franklin**. This example was printed on a tea cup without handles. The most unusual print, and probably giving the strongest voice to the notion of romantic death, was produced by Enoch Wood & Sons and titled **Washington Standing By His Own Tomb With A Scroll In His Hand**.

The existance of both the Romantic and Garden Cemetery movements explains several unusual historical Staffordshire prints. Neither George Washington nor Benjamin Franklin would have ever expected anyone to spend time ruminating over their graves. Yet Enoch Wood & Sons in both **Franklin's Tomb** and **Washington's Tomb** depict General Lafayette reclining by urn capped tombs, following the new nineteenth century custom and drawing inspiration from the resting places of his departed allies. Edward and George Phillips (1822-1834) show a young couple gazing at a tomb in an open glade in their print **Franklin**. Moral lessons were also supposed to be gained from grave-side ruminations. This example was printed on a tea cup without handles. The most unusual print, and probably giving the strongest voice to the notion of romantic death, was produced by Enoch Wood & Sons and titled **Washington Standing By His Own Tomb With A Scroll In His Hand**. The sugar bowl bearing this odd image measures 6 3/4" high. *Courtesy of the Collection of William R. & Teresa F. Kurau.*

The potters Ralph Stevenson and Williams of Cobridge provide a glimpse of yet another development of nineteenth century American social life, the museum, with their print Scudder's American Museum, located on Broadway in New York City. Early museums, in most cases, were as much a matter of showmanship as research. They were also frowned upon by most clergymen.[19]

Early American museums were as much a matter of showmanship as research. This is particularly true of the institution depicted here, Scudder's **American Museum**. Established by the Tammany Society in 1791, sold to Dr. Scudder in 1810, and later sold to P. T. Barnum in 1842, this institution surely fit the British description of an American museum to a tea, "...the greatest puerilities and absurdities in the world ...". The 7 1/8" diameter plate and print were produced by Ralph Stevenson and Williams c. 1825. *Courtesy of the Collection of William R. & Teresa F. Kurau.*

Scudder's American Museum was established by the Tammany Society in 1791 "for the purpose of collecting and preserving whatever may relate to the history of this country and also all other curiosities of nature and art." The scholarly caliber of these exhibits is best illustrated by a 1793 advertisement by the Society proclaiming an exhibition of live animals from South America and the Orient as well as an American grey squirrel "...in a machine in which he grinds pepper for his living."[20]

The Tammany Society soon lost interest in such lofty pursuits, selling the museum to Dr. Scudder in 1810. He, in turn, would sell the collection to Phineas Taylor Barnum, showman extraordinary, in 1842. Barnum had already established himself in the late 1830s with traveling shows filled with curiosities. These were on the upswing with the improvement of transportation systems across the nation, much to the consternation of clergymen everywhere. Despite ministerial disdain, traveling shows and museums were popular, especially among those who had little interest in prayer meetings, temperance hotels, and lyceum lectures.

Frederick Marryat, another traveling British author, would describe American museums collections in 1837 in less than glowing terms, "you have the greatest puerilities and absurdities in the world ...[and] you invariably have a large collection of daubs, called portraits of eminent personages, one-half of whom a stranger never heard of." Even more withering, a later British traveler spat out the following definition:

"A 'museum' in the American sense of the word means a place of amusement, wherein there shall be a theater, some wax figures, a giant and a dwarf or two, a jumble of pictures, and a few live snakes. In order that there may be some excuse for the use of the word, there is in most instances a collection of stuffed birds, a few preserved animals, and a stock of oddly assorted and very dubitable curiosities."

It is interesting to note, in light of the poor estimation in which this British traveler held American museology, that the one museum Ralph Stevenson and Williams chose to immortalize on dining wares was the American Museum purchased by Barnum. Surely it fit the English traveler's definition of an American museum perfectly.[21]

Transportation

Technological innovation during the nineteenth century vastly improved the lives of Americans over those of their predecessors. A doctrine of progress (with the appealing message that by forever moving forward perpetual improvement for all involved could be achieved) arose and excited the nation. Growing transportation technologies were seen as powerful tools of American progress, waterways and railroads supporting most of the transportation needs of a growing nation. The new transportation systems were also seen as improving lives by providing ever growing numbers of consumers greater access to manufactured goods.[22]

Staffordshire prints present a number of representations of steamboats, canals and canal barges, and railroads — symbols of progress all. On August 17, 1807, Robert Fulton introduced America to his *Steamboat*, the first practical operating steam-powered ship. He sailed it from it's Greenwich Village berth and chugged up river at 4 1/2 miles and hour, belching coal smoke, and navigating the New York City to Albany, New York run in thirty-two hours. This trip took sailing sloops four days to complete. While most were impressed, a Hudson River Valley farmer quipped that the *Steamboat* looked like "the devil going up the river in a sawmill."[23]

James and Thomas Edwards of Burslem provided Americans with a pleasant view of steamship transportation in their Boston Mails prints. The borders of their prints featured majestic images of the steam-packets Acadia, Britannia, Caledonia and Columbia cutting the waves. One seafaring traveler in the 1840s quickly discovered the difference between romantic image and reality upon entering his shipboard stateroom aboard the Britannia. He grumbled, "...this utterly impracticable, thoroughly hopeless, and profoundly preposterous box, had [only] the remotest reference to, or connexion with, those chaste and pretty, not to say gorgeous little bowers, sketched by a masterly hand ...".[24]

James and Thomas Edwards (1839-1841) created a deceptively luxurious image of steam ship travel with their Boston Mail series. This view is entitled the **Ladies Cabin** and appears on a 10" diameter plate. *Courtesy of the Collection of William R. & Teresa F. Kurau.*

Historical Staffordshire also commemorated travel and commerce on the Erie Canal. The Erie Canal was excavated and constructed across the wilds of northern New York state between Albany and Buffalo. Work on the waterway progressed from 1817 when construction began to 1825 when the canal opened. The 360 mile long artificial waterway connected Lake Erie and the Hudson River, opening trade between New York and the midwestern states while aiding in the growth of New York City as a port.[25]

The Erie Canal, scoffed at by Thomas Jefferson and supported by future Governor DeWitt Clinton, first linked the east coast and the mid-West prior to rail transport and helped establish New York City as a major port town. This important commercial causeway was commemorated by Enoch Wood & Sons with a series of Erie Canal prints including the **Entrance to the Erie Canal Into The Hudson At Albany**, shown here on a 6" diameter plate. *Courtesy of the Collection of William R. & Teresa F. Kurau.*

DeWitt Clinton, a former mayor of New York, was a strong supporter of the massive canal project, despite strong criticism from nay-sayers. Thomas Jefferson had declared the project "Little short of madness." During construction the canal was commonly referred to as the "Big Ditch;" afterwards, it was the "Grand Canal." Clinton's belief in the project was vindicated and in 1825, when the canal opened, he was the governor of the state of New York. No doubt the Staffordshire wares featuring the Erie Canal and Governor Clinton's portrait pleased him no end.[26]

As the century progressed, once steamships —— whatever their accommodations —— dropped their passengers off at port, their journey could proceeded (if not by canal barge) by train. Railroads were wending their way across a large portion of the American landscape by the mid-nineteenth century. America's first practical railroad was the Baltimore and Ohio. The B. & O. began passenger service on a mile-and-a-half long track outside of Baltimore, between Mount Clare and the Carrollton Viaduct, in 1830. Riders paid nine cents for the wildly popular round trip excursion.[27]

Enoch Wood & Sons produced two transfer printed views of the Baltimore & Ohio Railroad. However, the tiny engine in the print —- developed by George Stephenson in 1825 —- was never used in America. The late-nineteenth century author R. T. Haines Halsey believed this inaccuracy indicated the print was produced prior to the completion of the rail line in commemoration of the laying of the B. & O.'s first rail on July 4, 1828.[28]

The Boston Gazette, in July of 1830, expounded on the wonders of rail travel on the new B. & O. line, "In the hottest time of the hottest days the quick motion of the cars caused a current of air which renders the ride at all times agreeable. ... We only repeat the general sentiment when we say, it is the most delightful of all kinds of traveling." Michael Chevalier, a French writer traveling in America in 1838 further noted "...there is a perfect mania in this country on the subject of railroads...offering the ever-impatient Americans the service of their rapid cars at the points where the steamboats leave their passengers."

Baltimore & Ohio Railroad (Level) 10" diameter plate by Wood & Sons shows the early American railroad as it began to traverse the country and revolutionize nineteenth century life. The first American passenger train, the Tom Thumb, went into service in 1830. By 1838 the French writer Michael Chevalier would remark "...there is a perfect mania in this country on the subject of railroads...offering the ever-impatient Americans the service of their rapid cars at the points where the steamboats leave their passengers." *Courtesy of the Collection of William R. & Teresa F. Kurau.*

By 1840 an expanding network of roads, railroad lines and canals linked the major industrial and commercial centers of the United States. These were located in the northeastern and mid-Atlantic states.[29]

With steamboats, railroads and canals came greater access to imported goods than had been enjoyed before. New markets opened, demand increased, lifestyles changed. Trade in historical Staffordshire flourished under these conditions.

The Changing American Family

The social structure of family life changed as radically in the nineteenth century as the physical surroundings and these changes are reflected in the decorations on Staffordshire wares. Between 1780 and 1850 urban oriented wage labor replaced rural collective family labor. While husbands worked outside the home, their wives came to rule over domestic affairs.[30]

As a result, women were selecting furnishings and directing home affairs to an extent previously unknown. In circumstances where women were without children, opportunities for income-earning labor improved. This situation dramatically increased the resources of a couple and allowed them to purchase wares, including historical Staffordshire, that would have been beyond their parents' means in the eighteenth century. English women in pottery factories were applying the transfer prints on the Staffordshire wares and American women were selecting them for use at home.[31]

One of the most significant changes for many families during this period concerned their eating habits. During the eighteenth century the average family would have either eaten from wooden bowls and trenchers or "in common", that is, each member spooning food straight from a single central bowl.[32]

By 1800 few families were practicing communal eating. Considered to be one of the ruder aspects of the agrarian past, most were willing to abandon and forget the practice. Individualized social eating, providing each diner with a certain autonomy and privacy, was on the rise in which each member of the family had their own place setting and individual portions of food.

Additionally, improved transportation systems were enabling a greater diversity of foods to be available and the need for a wider variety of wares for the presentation of it. As the Victorian era progressed, dining would develop into a complex social ritual replete with many specialized dining wares and instruction manuals suggesting their proper usage.[33]

English mass production techniques accommodated these changes easily and provided matched sets of dishes. A ritual well established by 1800 was the tea ceremony. While tea previously had been a luxury item, by 1800 at least half of all American households had a teapot. For the first four decades of the nineteenth century, tea drinking increased steadily in America. However, by mid-century, tea was replaced by coffee, a stronger stimulant with a more powerful flavor. During the American Civil War (1861-1865) coffee was known to be the preferred drink of both the Union and Confederate armies.[34]

Historical Staffordshire prints could be inspirational and educational. They could even be used as a successful campaigning tool for presidential election. William Henry Harrison in 1840 successfully campaigned without substance on a platform emphasizing his links with the common man and his heroic military past. The **Columbian Star** pattern by J. & W. Ridgway, produced for the campaign, associated Harrison with the rustic log cabin of the common man. Two of the three possible views of the log cabin nineteenth century politicians were so ready to associate themselves with are presented here on the 6" x 6" sugar bowl and the 9" plate. *Courtesy of the Collection of William R. & Teresa F. Kurau.*

By 1800 at least half of all American households had a teapot and through the 1840s tea drinking would continue to rise. **Lafayette At Franklin's Tomb** teapot by Enoch Wood and Sons measuring 7 1/4" high. *Courtesy of the Collection of William R. & Teresa F. Kurau.*

Tea cup without a handle and with a large saucer, in vogue in the 1820s and 1830s. This design emulated the popular Chinese export porcelains in design. The hot tea was poured from the cup into the large saucer to cool. The cooling drink was sipped from the saucer. **The Landing Of General Lafayette At Castle Garden, New York, 16 August, 1824** by James and Ralph Clews. *Courtesy of the Collection of William R. & Teresa F. Kurau.*

Pictorial art, a source of inspiration for the private viewer and for pottery engravers, was largely absent from American homes prior to 1850. Only the wealthiest could manage to hang art on the walls, and most of those were portraits. The most likely place to find art, therefore, in the average home was on the dinner table or in the cupboards. Transfer prints, including those on historical Staffordshire wares, were providing thousands of homes with depictions of American, English, European and Oriental views where nothing but small wood cuts and engravings in books had been seen before. The impact of these images could be very strong. For example, in 1791, Irish convicts sent to Australia who escaped inland believed they could find a route to China. There they expected to find blue bridges and willows just like the ones on willow ware plates they had seen at home.[35]

Cadmus (so-called) cup plate by Enoch Wood & Sons, named for the ship which brought General Lafayette to America in 1824. The tea cup of the 1820s and 1830s was placed on a cup plate while tea cooled in the saucer. *Courtesy of the Collection of William R. & Teresa F. Kurau.*

The most likely place to find pictorial art in the average American home before 1850 was in the cupboards or on the dining tables. Historical Staffordshire prints were perfect for filling the void, providing a wide variety of domestic and foreign views. James & Ralph Clews provided a series of "Picturesque Views" in a variety of colors including this example titled **New York, Hudson River** on a platter measuring 21 3/4" X 17 1/2". *Courtesy of the Collection of William R. & Teresa F. Kurau.*

Commodore MacDonnough's Victory 11" high coffee pot with **Wadsworth Tower** printed on the lid. This was produced by Enoch Wood & Sons. Coffee replaced tea as the American drink of choice by the mid-nineteenth century. Tea cups without handles were also replaced with handled models with smaller saucers. Hot drinks were more manageable with a handled cup, saucers were no longer used to cool drinks and cup plates ceased to be used. *Courtesy of the Collection of William R. & Teresa F. Kurau.*

One sign of an up-and-coming family during the early decades of the nineteenth century was the presence of a chamber pot in each bed chamber to ward off night time shambles or mad dashes in rain or snow to distant outhouses. These pots were produced in a variety of low cost English wares. However, complete wash (or chamber) sets, a mark of gentility, included a matching basin and ewer, a soap-dish, and a sponge-dish for private bathing, a cup for brushing teeth, a slop pail and a chamber pot complete with a cover to reduce disagreeable odors and spillage. Examples of these wares in historical Staffordshire may be found. By mid-century chamber sets in every bed chamber would become more common and these sets remained a staple of the earthenware trade.[36]

American life would continue to change throughout the century. After 1850 new opportunities opened for increased income across a broad spectrum of society which came to view elaborate, ritualized behavior as a sign of sophistication.

With this change, demands for more elaborate formal dining wares grew and demand for historical Staffordshire fell. By 1860 the height of the wares' popularity had passed.

Part of the complete chamber set was the wash basin and pitcher. If a complete chamber set were present in every bed chamber, it was considered to be a sign of a family with rising fortunes during the first half of the nineteenth century. Produced by John Rogers & Sons (1818-1842), this wash basin and pitcher was decorated with the **Boston State House** view. This bowl and pitcher were small and intended for washing the face alone. The bowl measures 4 3/4" high and 12" in diameter; the pitcher measures 7 1/4" in diameter. *Courtesy of the Collection of William R. & Teresa F. Kurau.*

A larger wash pitcher and basin designed to bath more than the face. The 9" high pitcher is decorated with the vine bordered view **Esplanade And Castle Garden, New York**. The 13 1/2" diameter bowl is decorated with the vine bordered view **Lawrence Mansion** (so called). The set was produced by Ralph Stevenson. The view in the wash basin, better viewed in Chapter 5, is actually of the Boston Athenaeum with the spire of the Octagon Church behind it. *Courtesy of the Collection of William R. & Teresa F. Kurau.*

Chapter Three

Transfer Printing and Historical Staffordshire

Artisans and Their Subjects

The single most crucial design element of an historical Staffordshire ware was the transfer printed pattern. The quality of that pattern would largely decide whether the ware sold well or was largely ignored. Transfer printed patterns were created by artisans, some greatly skilled and others not so capable. The largest pottery manufacturers hired their own artist engravers. Smaller companies purchased their patterns from engraving firms. The artists who engraved the copper plates necessary for transfer printing occasionally became famous. One of their designs could become extremely popular. The acclaim and demand for that pattern would result in copies in many forms with many variations on the theme by other engravers. Prior to 1842, there were no copyright laws in England. Materials taken from current books and from competing engravers' works were common. The Stevenson's Cobridge works used the compiled views of the *Hudson River Port Folio* by the Irish artist W.G. Wall to great effect. Wall had been commissioned to collect the material during his 1818 visit to the United States for use on export wares and was recognized by name in the printed back marks on Stevenson's dinnerwares. A few popular transfer printed patterns, such as Thomas Minton's Willow pattern, remain popular today.[1]

Prior to 1842, there was no copyright law in England. Art was regularly taken from current books, prints and the works of other engravers to create new transfer prints. Here is Ralph Stevenson's **The Battle of Bunker Hill** with a copy of the original art work. *Courtesy of the Collection of William R. & Teresa F. Kurau.*

The Stevenson's Cobridge works used the compiled views of the Hudson River Port Folio by the Irish artist W. G. Wall for their views. Andrew Stevenson produced this copy of a W. G. Wall work in transfer print, **Church And Buildings Adjoining Murray Street, New York**. He even attributed the view to the artist in the back mark. *Courtesy of the Collection of William R. & Teresa F. Kurau.*

The early English transfer prints were mostly chinoiseries, copying the success of the Chinese import porcelains. Shortly afterwards, European elements were added to the designs to make them more familiar to the western market. Western touches included floral borders surrounding Chinese scenes. Later patterns would begin to mix Oriental, Egyptian and Western motifs into a veritable design stew for the central prints on ceramics. Between roughly 1815 and 1835, large export markets opened for England in North America, Europe, India and other countries. By this time patterns included the familiar patriotic themes and views from engravings of contemporary artists found on historical Staffordshire in America. Borders were used during this period to identify pieces of a single service with more than one central pattern.[2]

The British Copyright Act of 1842 slowly brought to an end the habit of copying the works of other engravers, usually with nothing changed but the name of the piece, or the art work in books. If the work was registered, it was not to be copied. This brought about a rise in generic landscapes featuring some combination of mountains with water, trees, exotic architecture, and small, nondescript human figures engaged in pleasant pastimes. These were sometimes given place names; however, the printed image rarely resembled the named location.[3]

Production of Transfer Prints

Transfer printing became a respected and powerful mass production tool. It enabled a pottery to reproduce many copies of the same pattern quickly with the aid of predominantly semi-skilled laborers, and without the expense of employing trained artists. Historical Staffordshire ceramics were decorated with transfer printed designs under the final clear glaze surface so that the patterns were sealed and could not wear off with frequent use.

To create the transfer prints, engravers designed or adapted a suitable design to the shape of the pieces to be decorated. The design was then inscribed in to a flat sheet of copper by cutting or etching lines or dots into the copper. The deeper or thicker the line or dot, or the closer these were placed together, the darker would be the final color. When the engraving was completed there was a different copper plate prepared for each size or shape of ceramic to be decorated. The copper plate was warmed to prepare it for the application of ceramic pigment.[4]

Once heated, the plate was ready for the application of a thick oily ceramic pigment, originally a deep cobalt blue was used. As the name suggests, the blue pigment color was obtained from the mineral cobalt. Cobalt blue was the first color discovered during eighteenth century experimentation with underglazing which would tolerate the high temperatures required to fire a glaze on a ceramic body. It was in common use by 1776.[5]

The ceramic pigment was rubbed into the recessed design. Excess pigment was removed from the plate with a palette knife, and the surface of the copper plate was then rubbed clean. Only the recesses of the engraved design re-

mained filled with pigment and the plate was now considered "charged" and ready for use.[6]

At this point a special, soft, pliable, strong tissue-like transfer paper was applied to the heated and charged copper plate, and both were placed under an even pressure with a felt pad. The pressure transferred the pigment to the paper, which was then lifted from the copper plate and passed to a worker who cut away the excess paper.

Once the paper was prepared, the cut and charged paper was carefully positioned onto the unglazed ceramic (bisque) body and rubbed down with soft-soap flannels. The ware with the paper attached was then immersed in cold water causing the ink to stiffen and the paper to float away, leaving the pigment design behind on the ceramic body.[7]

Usually women were responsible for the meticulous work of placing the pattern correctly and for joining the seams of the borders and designs. The care with which the women who applied the transfer prints is often evident. They were aware of the nineteenth century Victorian ideal of the "perfect finish." This finish was defined as either work with great realistic detail and meticulous surface finish or the concealment of the methods of production used to obtain the finished result. Many of the historical Staffordshire prints show these ladies tried hard to meet the ideal.[8]

The manufacturer's mark, often incorporating the name given to the transfer printed pattern, was engraved on the same copper plate as the main design. These were laid down at the same time as the main pattern. The manufacturer's mark usually provided the pattern name, the initials or name of the maker and in many cases the town where the factory was located. Once transferred to the paper the mark was cut off and applied to the backs of plates or to the bases of hollow wares. Marks were omitted at times for a variety of reasons.[9]

While these marks are one of the best and easiest clues in identifying a piece, a few of them will always remain a mystery. There were so many manufacturers, producing such enormous quantities of wares that not all the marks were identified. Also, some potters stayed in business for such a short time and made so few pieces that the identity of their marks have been lost to history. Additionally, many small firms either saw no reason to use marks as these tiny manufacturer's had no name recognition value.[10]

Once the transfer paper was applied to the body and the paper had been soaked off, the ware was then lightly fired to burn off the oil in the pigment. Next the body was dipped in a final, clear glaze and fired at a high heat, sealing the print under the glaze.[11]

Transfer printed designs were used only when a relatively long run of a particular design was required. No one went to the expense of engraving a copper plate for a single object or even a small run and no one ever engraved a costly set of coppers for a service, if only a few were to be made. With these restrictions it is easy to see that no printed design was ever unique. There were no one-of-a-kind issues in transfer printing.[12]

The women who applied the transfer prints frequently strove to meet the nineteenth century ideal of a perfect finish, in this case a concealment of the methods of production used to obtain the finished results. The **View of Newburgh**, New York by Job and John Jackson meets this ideal. The view adorns a platter measuring 17 1/2" X 14 3/4". *Courtesy of the Collection of William R. & Teresa F. Kurau.*

Peculiarities of the Wares

While transfer printed wares are examples of early mass production, the patterns were still applied by hand. Individuals placed them and the results were not always perfect. It is interesting to search for signs of individuality when looking at historical Staffordshire ceramics.

When matching transfer papers to wares, individual sections were often cut out and fit to the shape of the wares. The match lines are often visible. More interesting is what happens to transfer printed wares containing inscriptions. Hastily engraved copper plates provided transfers that had to be cut and trimmed to fit vessels of different sizes. The trimming and fitting process often led to nearly illegible inscriptions as letters were cropped off here and there. Pictures often remained whole but words suffered, not that it mattered to the women fitting the pattern; few of them could read. For that matter, many of the customers could not read either.[13]

Transfer printing also was a messy job. The ink did get on the hands of the women transferring the designs to the wares. Occasionally you may discover a finger or thumb print on the back of a plate from the original transferrer. This will be the only truly unique pattern you will ever find on transfer printed wares. If there are no finger prints, there may be imprints of other pieces on the bases of flat wares such as plates or platters or, on earlier wares, there may be stilt marks.

Stilt marks consist of three small dots in the glaze made by triangular spur pieces (stilts) which separated the flat wares in early nineteenth century kilns. Later in the nineteenth century, different measures were taken to separate the plates in the kilns and stilt marks disappeared.

Hastily engraved copper plates provided transfers that had to be cut and trimmed to fit various sized vessels. The trimming often lead to virtually illegible inscriptions as letters were cropped. Pictures often remained whole but words suffered as few of the women trimming the prints could read. They trimmed that which had little meaning to them. Not that it mattered too much, many of the customers could not read either. **Lafayette at Franklin's Tomb** coffee pot by Enoch Wood & Sons, note the way Franklin's name has been shortened to fit the transfer to the narrowing base of the pot. *Courtesy of the Collection of William R. & Teresa F. Kurau.*

Transfer printing was a messy job. The back of this **Arms of Pennsylvania** platter by Thomas Mayer was laid or fell directly on top of another printed but unfired platter decorated with the same print. That second print is now partially printed on the back of the platter. This platter measures 20 3/4" x 15 3/4". *Courtesy of the Collection of William R. & Teresa F. Kurau.*

Chapter Four

Dating and Identification of Historical Staffordshire

Identifiable and Datable Traits

When out searching for just the right historical Staffordshire piece to add to your collection, it is always useful to have a few guidelines for a quick identification and dating of an unusual, or occasionally unmarked, piece that catches your eye. We have already discussed in detail the various body types you will encounter (creamware, pearlware, ironstone and it's cousins, and porcelain). Further dating clues come from the color of the transfer print, the design of the print itself, border designs, the manufacturers' marks which always contain useful information, and the registration marks and numbers employed on British ceramics after the Copyright Act of 1842. A basic understanding of these will provide you with valuable insights concerning any piece you wish to examine.

The Color of the Transfer Print

The colors of the transfer prints are useful indicators of particular time periods. By 1818 a craze for very dark blue printed wares was on the rise in America. The Staffordshire potters were quick to respond, providing series with dark blue prints. Many of these were actually negative patterns with the subjects of the view left in white while the background was filled with dark blue. Dark blue patterns would remain popular throughout the 1820s.[1]

Brown printed pearlwares were being imported into the American market as early as 1809. In 1828 underglaze techniques were developed to transfer black, green, yellow and red enamels, allowing for the creation of new colored prints and prints with two colors. In 1829 Simeon Shaw noted that very recently several potters had introduced red, green and brown transfer printed patterns. American archaeologist and nineteenth century ceramics expert George Miller found that potters' "...invoices from 1829 into the 1840s listed quantities of red, green, brown, and purple printed wares." These printed patterns were on white wares.[2]

The early deep cobalt blue color, so popular in the 1820s, was changed around 1845 when coarser synthetic blues were introduced. In 1848 multiple color underglazing techniques were further developed by F. Collins and A. Reynolds of Hanley, allowing three colors, red, yellow and blue, to be applied in a single transfer with only one firing. Green and brown were added in 1852 and the process was used into the 1860s.[3]

The popularity of transfer printed wares generally declined in the 1850s, being replace by white granite wares. Demand for printed wares rose again in the early 1870s. By this time historical Staffordshire prints were on a rapid decline, having been replaced by wares more in keeping with changing artistic and social movements of the period.[4]

By 1818 a craze for very dark blue printed wares was on the rise in America. Several example of these popular dark blue prints: two **Landing Of General Lafayette At Castle Gardens, New York, 16 August, 1824** 4 5/8" cup plates by James and Ralph Clews and one large 18 1/2" x 14 1/2" well and tree platter by Enoch Wood and Sons adorned with the print **Christianburg, Danish Settlement On The Gold Coast, Africa**. *Courtesy of the Collection of William R. & Teresa F. Kurau.*

By 1829 several Staffordshire potters had introduced red, green, brown and purple transfer printed patterns. Examples include: **City Hall, Albany**, a 10 1/2" diameter plate by Ralph Stevenson, the **Episcopal Theological Seminary, Lexington, Kentucky** by an unknown manufacturer on a 10 1/2" diameter plate and a portion of a **Harvard College** view by Job & John Jackson in brown on a cup plate measuring 4 5/8" in diameter. *Courtesy of the Collection of William R. & Teresa F. Kurau.*

Multiple color underglazing techniques were refined in 1848, allowing three colors (red, yellow and blue) to be applied in a single transfer. In 1852 additional colors (green and brown) were added. The results could be stunning as in these Landing Of General Lafayette At Castle Garden, New York, 16 August, 1824 views on a 8 5/8" pitcher and a twin handled dish measuring 17". Neither has a manufacturer's mark for identification. *Courtesy of the Collection of William R. & Teresa F. Kurau.*

Periods of Transfer Print Production

1780-1815

Between roughly 1780 and 1815 experimentation led to successful underglazed transfer printing techniques. The earliest printed patterns were copies of the popular Chinese export porcelains. The early prints were etched into the copper plates with simple line engraving techniques. As a result, the plates held a great deal of ink and the prints produced were dark and at times slightly blurred. From 1800-1815 transfer printing skills improved. Line engraving was combined with stippling which allowed for the creation of shadows, clouds and other delicate shadings.[5]

Between 1800-1815, Chinese designs were still prominent. However, European motifs also were slipping into the works as flowered borders and European architectural features cropped up. The chinoiseries became more standardized as well, leading to the Willow pattern. Also a search for more interesting material was leading British potters to use designs from illustrated books and topographical views of exotic lands, botanical magazines, and political satire.[6]

1815-1835

After disengaging from various military entanglements around 1815, Britain enjoyed a tremendous upswing in demand for transfer printed earthenwares. Markets opened up in North America, Europe, India and elsewhere. Even the home market grew. Very few potters were not involved in this lucrative trade. This was a period of patriots and the picturesque for the American market.

In England, William Gilpin (1724-1804), a Hampshire clergyman, toured England and wrote a series of books on scenery and illustrated them with aquatints. His books sparked the "cult of the picturesque" in England, leading to an avalanche of more illustrated scenic books. While Gilpin's tour and resultant cult were lampooned around 1810 in a farcical series entitled "Doctor Syntax in Search of the Picturesque," these illustrated works provided a treasure trove of materials for potters willing to ride on their popular appeal.[7]

Dinner wares were produced with several series of titled patterns such as James and Ralph Clews' "Cities Series" or John and William Ridgway's "Beauties of America." Such patterns were almost always surrounded with borders, mainly floral and frequently enclosing smaller designs in medallions within the borders. The same border pattern (ensconced on plate and dish rims, edges of mugs, tureens and other wares) was used for a complete dinner service. Some manufacturers regarded these borders as their unique trademarks but not all manufacturers' respected that idea. Both borders and central patterns were copied from time-to-time. However, by familiarizing yourself with the border designs presented on the wares in Chapter 5 and identified by the manufacturers, you will have a good general guide as to which borders were employed by specific manufacturers.[8]

Dinner wares were produced in series of titled patterns such as James and Ralph Clews "Cities Series" or John and William Ridgway's "Beauties of America." From Clews Cities Series, the pattern **Albany** on a 10" diameter bowl. From the Ridgways Beauties of America series, the pattern **Bank, Savannah** printed on the outside of a 9 3/4" diameter, 5 1/4" high fruit compote. *Courtesy of the Collection of William R. & Teresa F. Kurau.*

1835-1845

During this period, a variety of colors other than blue were employed in transfer prints as their development techniques improved. However, by this period the middle class consumers interested in transfer printed earthenwares had already purchased their dining services and other useful wares. Being durable, the wares lasted for years so cheaper services began to be produced to reach consumers with less financial means, the mill workers and farm laborers for example. As the quality of these lesser wares was declining, the patterns were becoming more standardized and the less creative work was less expensive. Yet there was still a range of earthenwares with transfer printed designs produced. Some manufacturers maintained higher standards than others. Still, the trend was towards the less expensive wares.[9]

A further restriction on creative work was imposed —
- or at least on creative copying. The Copyright Act of 1842
protected registered original designs from copying for three
years. This effectively stripped the Staffordshire potters of
much of their source materials, such as books filled with
illustrations.[10]

As a result, coupled with the rise of the Romantic Movement, potters turned to formulaic romantic scenes to fill
the void. The proscribed romantic scene included most often a centrally located body of water, either a lake or a river.
To one side should stand some edifice of classical architecture, the nationality of which was up to the engraver to de-
termine while considering his targeted market. On the other
side of the water should be a large tree in the foreground.
Beneath the tree an urn, a fountain or a pillared balcony
should rest. Mountains in the background and people in the
foreground were recommended. A family dog was sometimes helpful. At times these scenes bore the titles of real
towns and rivers, however, the image rarely corresponded
to reality.[11]

In spite of the distinct lack of imagination in these romantic patterns, the quality of some to the transfer printed
earthenwares remained high.

Despite a mild upsurge in interest in transfer printed
earthenwares during the 1870s, these wares were in steady
decline over the second half of the nineteenth century. The
number of new patterns produced was dwindling. White
dinner services with simple printed borders were replacing
printed decorations which covered the entire surface. Other
wares and different decorative techniques were overtaking
them.[12]

Dating Historical Staffordshire with Manufactur-ers' Marks and Components of the Marks.

Almost always visible on the underside or along the
bottom of historical Staffordshire wares is the name given
to the central pattern. While this is interesting, far more
informative are the manufacturers' marks which accompany
these names from time-to-time. Manufacturers' marks first-
and-foremost identify the potter by name and frequently
include both the symbol and city location of the firm. For a
firm with a long history, these marks are particularly helpful in dating the marked wares as they were periodically
changed and the marks of each particular period are usually well recorded.

As a result of the Copyright law of 1842 in England,
potters turned away from book illustrations toward
formulaic romantic scenes to create their transfers.
**The Valley Of The Shenandoah From Jefferson's
Rock** by William Ridgway has most, if not all, of
the elements necessary for a proper romantic scene.
The plate measures 7" in diameter. *Courtesy of the
Collection of William R. & Teresa F. Kurau.*

Manufacturer's marks identify the potter by name
and frequently include both the symbol and city
location of the firm. Enoch Wood & Sons impressed
manufacturer's mark complete with body type name
Semi China and the Burslem city location of the
pottery. This mark with the spread eagle symbol was
used from 1818-1846 on finely printed wares made
for the American market. *Courtesy of the Collection of William R. & Teresa F. Kurau.*

Manufacturers' marks take on a variety of forms from scratchings and impressed or stamped marks in the soft body prior to firing to painted or transfer printed marks above or beneath the glaze. The impressed and the transfer printed marks are the most common on historical Staffordshire.

With a little additional knowledge as to the date of appearance of specific features on manufacturers' marks, additional information may be wrung from them. The guidelines which follow provide key elements and their dates of introduction on British marks.

All printed marks occur after 1800	1800
Marks incorporating the name of the pattern postdate 1810	1810
The English Royal Coat of Arms appear on marks after 1810	1810
"Published by," a term in use from c. 1830 to 1840 referring to the English 1797 Sculpture Copyright Act.	1830
Victorian quarter arms appear in 1838	1838
Round or oval shaped garter-like marks appear in 1840	1840
Diamond-shaped registration marks are applied along with manufacturers' marks in 1842 in compliance with the Copyright Act of that year and cease to be used after 1883.	1842
"Royal" becomes a common term attached to many manufacturer's trade names after 1850.	1850
"Limited" or it's abbreviation (Ltd.) is incorporated into English manufacturers' marks in 1860 and beyond after an English act of law establishes them in 1855.	1860
"Trade Mark" has been applied to English wares from 1863 onward in accordance with the Trademark Act of 1862.	1863
"Copyright reserved," a legal term on English wares, appears on English marks from 1877 onward.	1877
"England" appears in marks post-dating 1880, and generally after 1891, on export wares.	1880
Registration numbers replaced the diamond shaped registration marks in 1884 as proof of the registration of a design or process. Wares featuring these Rd No. marks are beyond our period of investigation.	1884 [13]

Registration Marks and Registration Numbers

For any piece of historical Staffordshire post-dating 1842, English registration marks are possibly the most complete and useful marks for dating ceramics. Since 1842, English decorative art designs were registered at the British patent office, seriously limiting the range of subjects produced on historical Staffordshire wares. However, not every registered piece was marked.[14]

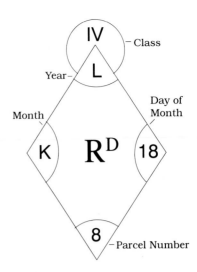

**Registration Mark
1842-1867**

A diamond-shaped registry mark was used between 1842 and 1883. The layout of the information within the diamond was altered after 1867. In 1884 the diamond-shaped marks were replace with simple and less informative registry numbers. Registry numbers (Rd. No.) indicated the year the marked piece was registered in a numeric sequence beginning in 1884 with the number 1. Any of these systems provide the earliest possible date of manufacture for the marked ware.[15]

The diamond-shaped registry marks in use from 1842-1867 contained a series of letters and numbers with the following meanings:

the large Rd was the abbreviation for "registered"

the Roman numeral in the circle above the apex of the diamond mark represented the type of material used in the production of the marked ware

the Roman numeral within the semi-circle below the apex of the diamond represented the year of registry

the Arabic numeral to the right of the Rd abbreviation represented the day of the month of registry

the Arabic numeral below the Rd abbreviation represented the parcel number, which was a code indicating the person or company who registered the pattern or the ware

the letter to the left of the Rd abbreviation represented the month of registry

In 1868, the numbers and their locations were adjusted as follows:

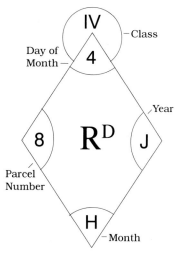

**Registration Mark
1868-1883**

TABLE 3
Year of Manufacture - 1842 - 1867

1842 - X	1851 - P	1860 - Z
1843 - H	1852 - D	1861 - R
1844 - C	1853 - Y	1862 - O
1845 - A	1854 - J	1863 - G
1846 - I	1855 - E	1864 - N
1847 - F	1856 - L	1865 - W
1848 - U	1857 - K	1866 - Q
1849 - S	1858 - B	1867 - T
1850 - V	1859 - M	

TABLE 4
Year of Manufacture - 1868 - 1883

1868 - X	1874 - U	1879 - Y
1869 - H	1875 - S	1880 - J
1870 - C	1876 - V	1881 - E
1871 - A	1877 - P	1882 - L
1872 - I	1878 - D	1883 - K
1873 - F		

the large Rd and the Roman numeral above the diamond remained unchanged

the Arabic numeral within the semi-circle below the apex of the diamond represented the day of the month of registry

the letter to the right of the Rd abbreviation represented the year of registry

the letter below the Rd abbreviation signified the month of registry

and the Arabic numeral to the left of the Rd abbreviation represented the parcel number.[16]

The tables below provide the meaning for the various code numbers and letters on the diamond-shaped registry marks.[17]

TABLE 1
Type of material or class

I - metal	II - wood
III - glass	IV - ceramics

TABLE 2
Month of the Year of Manufacture

C - January	I - July
G - February	R - August
W - March	D - September
H - April	B - October
E - May	K - November
M - June	A - December

After 1883, the diamond marks were discontinued in favor of a simpler marking system providing only the year of registration. This was the abbreviation "Rd No" followed by a number. This mark appears on decorative art manufactured in England after 1884 and may be found on late examples of historical Staffordshire wares by Minton and Company, Rowland and Marsellus Company, and Wedgwood.[18]

TABLE 5
Partial Guide to Design Registry Numbers 1884 - 1925 [19]

Year	1st Rd. No. of Each Year
1884	1
1885	20000
1890	142300
1895	248200
1900	351600
1905	447800
1909	548920
1915	644935
1920	673750
1925	710165

Manufacturers and Their Wares

The following is a survey of the Staffordshire potters and their historical Staffordshire wares. This presents a solid representative sample of what is available from the significant manufacturers of this popular ware. The series and their views produced by each manufacturer will be listed. The photographs present a representative sampling of these series and views.

The Adams Family

The Adams family produced a long and prodigious line of creative Staffordshire potters with an unfortunate lack of creativity in naming sons. They proclaim a 1657 date of establishment and continue to produce ceramic wares today. During the first half of the nineteenth century, three cousins named William Adams worked several Staffordshire potteries. The William Adams born in 1745, once apprenticed to Josiah Wedgwood, operated out of Greengates, Tunstall from 1779-1805. He produced a variety of earthenwares including blue jasper wares with white reliefs in the Wedgwood style. On his death in 1805, his son Benjamin Adams ran the Tunstall operation, turning out high quality blue transfer printed pearlware impressed B. ADAMS.[1]

William Adams, operating the Greenfield Works of Stoke-on-Trent from 1804-1829 specialized in blue transfer printed earthenware. Adams produced quality earthenwares enjoyed both in the home market and abroad. His offerings featured patriotic scenes and scenic views for export to the United States. The Stoke-on-Trent works may have been the first to employ a steam engine for the grinding of their flints. The ceramic wares produced at this factory were considered to be comparable in style and quality to Wedgwood's wares. The Stoke-on-Trent works would pass out of the Adams family's hands in 1863.[2]

William Adams and his sons William and Thomas, son and grandsons of William Adams of Stoke-on-Trent, operated the Greenfield Works of Tunstall, under the name William Adams and Sons and produced the historical Staffordshire wares presented here. The Greenfield Works were originally established in Stoke-on-Trent by William Adams' father who ran the works under his own name until 1829. In 1834 Greenfield opened new works at Tunstall with his son William at the helm. According the Llewellyn Jewitt, a ceramics historian writing in the late 1870s, the firm experienced a dissolution in 1853 and the works were continued by William Adams (the father of William and Thomas) until 1865, when he retired. In 1865 the firm passed to his sons, William and Thomas.[3]

The Greenfield Works concentrated on the export trade, producing wares for the United States, Central America, Brazil, Cuba, Manila, Singapore and other foreign markets. The Adams' wares from Greenfield Works consisted of tea and table services, toilet sets and other domestic wares bearing decorations Jewitt described as having a "...the bright fancy character of which is much admired in the out-markets of the world ..."[4]

Between the Stoke-on-Trent and Tunstall works, the following historical Staffordshire transfer printed series were produced. Of these the American Views and Columbus Views series were considered to be very successful.

Series and Views

American Views Series

Varied scenic views from around the United States printed in pink, brown and black. These are bordered with flowers, shells and scrolls. The views include:
Catskill Mountain House, U.S; Falls of Niagara, U.S.; Harper's Ferry, U.S.; Headwaters of the Juniata, U.S.; Lake George, U.S.; Military School, West Point, U.S.; Montevideo, Connecticut, U.S.; New York, U.S.; Skenectady on the Mohawk River, U.S.; Shannondale Springs, Virginia, U.S.; View Near Conway, New Hampshire, U.S.; White Mountains, New Hampshire, U.S.

Mark employed by William Adams & Sons for the pattern name in the American Views series. *Courtesy of the Collection of William R. & Teresa F. Kurau.*

Military School, West Point, N.Y., U.S. platter by William Adams & Sons, 17 1/2" x 14 3/4". *Courtesy of the Collection of William R. & Teresa F. Kurau.*

The Falls Of Niagara, U.S. platter by William Adams & Sons, 19 3/4" x 16 1/4". *Courtesy of the Collection of William R. & Teresa F. Kurau.*

Headwaters Of The Juniata, U.S. plate by William Adams & Sons, 10 1/4" in diameter. *Courtesy of the Collection of William R. & Teresa F. Kurau.*

Skenectady On The Mohawk River, U.S. dish by William Adams & Sons, 9 3/4" x 5 3/4" x 1 3/4" high. *Courtesy of the Collection of William R. & Teresa F. Kurau.*

Columbus Views Series

This series was comprised of eight scenes depicting the landing of Columbus and landscapes with Indians.

Mitchell & Freeman's China And Glass Warehouse, Chatham Street, Boston plate by William Adams, 10 1/4" in diameter. *Courtesy of the Collection of William R. & Teresa F. Kurau.*

Columbus plate by William Adams & Sons, 9 1/4" in diameter. *Courtesy of the Collection of William R. & Teresa F. Kurau.*

Printed pattern name mark used in the Columbus series and two manufacturer's marks. The printed mark features the initials W.A.&S. which was frequently used by the firm from 1819 to 1864. The impressed ADAMS mark was in use from 1800 to 1864 on earthenwares. *Courtesy of the Collection of William R. & Teresa F. Kurau.*

The Hudson River Views

These include three picturesque Hudson River scenes printed in pink and surrounded with a border of flowers, birds and scrolls. The views included:
Fairmount; Fort Edward, Hudson River; View Near Sandy Hill.

Log Cabin

A central view of William Henry Harrison's birth place, the standard log cabin presidential candidates were pleased to be able to harken back to, with border medallions of Major General W.H. Harrison and urns.

Mitchell & Freeman's China and Glass Warehouse, Chatham Street, Boston

Mitchell & Freeman, the central subject of this print, were in business from 1828 to 1832 and probably ordered this print themselves. Along with the warehouse is a view along Chatham Street to the distant upper harbor where several ships are docked. This view was printed in dark blue and surrounded with a border of trees and other flora.

Seal of the United States

This print featured the Great Seal of the United States surrounded by a border of flowers and scrolls and was printed in the dark blue so popular in the early nineteenth century. This print was produced by William Adams prior to his sons inclusion in the firm.

Seal Of The United States pitcher by William Adams, 6 3/4" high. *Courtesy of the Collection of William R. & Teresa F. Kurau.*

Individual views of both **Washington** and **New York** were also produced.

Marks

The Adams family marks usually incorporate the family name, Adams. W. Adams & Sons used W.A. & S. or the firm's full name. A variety of impressed and printed backstamps were produced. Blue transfer printed wares destined from the United States were impressed with an eagle and also bore the printed name of the subject in a foliate cartouche. After 1829 W. ADAMS & SONS is the manufacturers' mark in use.[5]

James & Ralph Clews

James and Ralph Clews rented the Cobridge Works in Cobridge, Staffordshire from William Adams in 1815. The brothers specialized in high quality blue transfer printed wares during their partnership, which ended in 1834. They produced several pattern series including some for the export trade to America and Russia. Particularly noteworthy among the exports to America for the quality of the transfer printing is the series entitled American Views. The favorite among Clews patterns exported to America, however, is The Landing of Lafayette at Castle Garden, New York, commemorating the general's return visit to the United States in 1824.[6]

While outside the scope of the current discussion, Clews produced several unique series. These were entitled the Doctor Syntax Series based on William Combe's books printed from 1815-1821 lampooning the "cult of the picturesque," the Wilkie's Designs Series (or Pictures of Sir David Wilkie) and the Zoological Series. These apparently sold better overseas than in England and would make a fine addition to another volume.[7]

After the dissolution of the firm in 1834, James Clews sailed for America, joining the Indiana Pottery Company of Troy, Indiana as one of three principals. He remained in the United States for five years.[8]

Series and Views

America and Independence Series

This is a dark blue printed series with a woman on either side of the central, frequently romantic, view. To the left the woman holds up an image of Washington. This woman is blindfolded, symbolic of justice. The kneeling woman to the right wears the Liberty Cap and holds the Liberty Pole. The names of fifteen states in festoons create the border. The largely romantic views are mostly given descriptive names including:
New York Customs House; Building, Deer On Lawn; Building, Fishermen With Net; Building, Sheep On Lawn; Mansion, Foreground A Lake With Swans; Three Story Mansion, Small Extension To Left; Three Story Building, Two Wings And Center Section; Two Story Building With Curved Drive; Building In Distance, Women In Foreground; Castle With Flag, Boats In Foreground; Mansion, Small Boat With Flag In Foreground; Building, Two Wings, Water In Foreground; Mansion, Circular Drive; Mansion, Winding Drive.

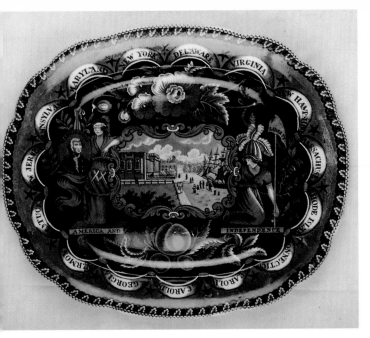

Mansion, a small boat with a flag in the foreground platter by James & Ralph Clews, 14 3/4" x 12 3/4". *Courtesy of the Collection of William R. & Teresa F. Kurau.*

New York Customs House platter by James & Ralph Clews, 19 1/4" x 16 1/4". *Courtesy of the Collection of William R. & Teresa F. Kurau.*

Building, sheep on the lawn plate by James & Ralph Clews, 8 1/2" in diameter. *Courtesy of the Collection of William R. & Teresa F. Kurau.*

Mansion, a small boat with a flag in the foreground fruit compote with missing loop handles by James & Ralph Clews, 5 1/4" x 11" x 8 1/2". The tureen is impressed with the manufacturer's mark "CLEWS WARRANTED STAFFORDSHIRE" with a crown which was in use from c. 1818 to 1834. *Courtesy of the Collection of William R. & Teresa F. Kurau.*

Building, two wings, water in foreground pitcher by James & Ralph Clews, 6 3/4" high. *Courtesy of the Collection of William R. & Teresa F. Kurau.*

American Eagle and Urn

This dark blue print featured an urn decorated with a variation of the Great Seal of the United States. Flowers and urns decorated the borders.

American Eagle On Urn creamer by James & Ralph Clews, 4 1/2" high. *Courtesy of the Collection of William R. & Teresa F. Kurau.*

City Series

Featuring a variety of views of both American and foreign cities in both a dark and a lighter blue. The border is composed of bouquets of flowers and scrolls. The cities included:
Albany; Baltimore; Buenos Ayres; Chillicothe (with cows); Chillicothe (with raft); Columbus; Detroit; Hobart Town; Louisville, Kentucky; Near Fishkill;   Philadelphia; Near Philadelphia; Quebec; Sandusky; Washington; Wright's Ferry On The Susquehanna; Unidentified Harbor View.

The printed title mark used for the Cities Series. *Courtesy of the Collection of William R. & Teresa F. Kurau.*

Albany bowl by James & Ralph Clews, 10" in diameter. *Courtesy of the Collection of William R. & Teresa F. Kurau.*

An interesting additional mark of a New Orleans based import house, Hill and Henderson. *Courtesy of the Collection of William R. & Teresa F. Kurau.*

Buenos Ayres plate by James & Ralph Clews, 10" in diameter. *Courtesy of the Collection of William R. & Teresa F. Kurau.*

Columbus platter by James & Ralph Clews, 14 3/4" x 11 1/2". *Courtesy of the Collection of William R. & Teresa F. Kurau.*

Buenos Ayres bowl with a view of **Quebec** on the outside of the bowl by James & Ralph Clews. *Courtesy of the Collection of William R. & Teresa F. Kurau.*

Hobart Town plate by James & Ralph Clews, 9" in diameter. *Courtesy of the Collection of William R. & Teresa F. Kurau.*

Louisville, Kentucky platter by James & Ralph Clews, 12 1/2" x 9 3/4". *Courtesy of the Collection of William R. & Teresa F. Kurau.*

Near Fishkill plate by James & Ralph Clews, 7 3/4" in diameter. *Courtesy of the Collection of William R. & Teresa F. Kurau.*

Quebec bowl by James & Ralph Clews, 9" in diameter. *Courtesy of the Collection of William R. & Teresa F. Kurau.*

A View Near Philadelphia soup bowl by James & Ralph Clews, 9 3/4" in diameter. *Courtesy of the Collection of William R. & Teresa F. Kurau.*

Quebec printed on the outside of this bowl with **Buenos Ayres** printed within by James & Ralph Clews. *Courtesy of the Collection of William R. & Teresa F. Kurau.*

Sandusky platter by James & Ralph Clews, 13 1/4" x 16 3/4". *Courtesy of the Collection of William R. & Teresa F. Kurau.*

Flowers and Foliage

These views of American buildings are surrounded by a border of flower chains and heavy foliage and were printed in dark blue. Views include:
City Hall, New York; Insane Asylum, New York; and three unidentified structures.

Insane Asylum, New York pitcher by James & Ralph Clews, 6 3/4" high. These two views are on opposite sides of the same pitcher. Several views on one piece are to be found from time-to-time. *Courtesy of the Collection of William R. & Teresa F. Kurau.*

Lafayette, The Nation's Guest

The central print is an oval medallion emblazoned with the smiling visage of General Lafayette printed in dark blue and simply bordered with either a narrow blue or green band on flatwares. Pitchers had a floral and scroll border.

City Hall, New York pitcher by James & Ralph Clews, 6 3/4" high. *Courtesy of the Collection of William R. & Teresa F. Kurau.*

Welcome Lafayette The Nation's Guest And Our Country's Glory pitcher by James & Ralph Clews, 7" high. *Courtesy of the Collection of William R. & Teresa F. Kurau.*

The Landing of Lafayette

A dark blue print commemorating the landing of General Lafayette at Castle Garden, New York in 1824. The print is surrounded by a border of flowers and vines.

The Landing Of General Lafayette At Castle Garden, New York, 16 August, 1824 platter by James & Ralph Clews, 19" x 14 3/4". *Courtesy of the Collection of William R. & Teresa F. Kurau.*

The Landing Of General Lafayette At Castle Garden, New York, 16 August, 1824 plate by James & Ralph Clews, 10" in diameter. *Courtesy of the Collection of William R. & Teresa F. Kurau.*

The Landing Of General Lafayette At Castle Garden, New York, 16 August, 1824 well-and-tree platter by James and Ralph Clews, 21" x 14 3/4". *Courtesy of the Collection of William R. & Teresa F. Kurau.*

The Landing Of General Lafayette At Castle Garden, New York, 16 August, 1824 vegetable dish by James & Ralph Clews, 10 1/2" x 8" x 2 1/4". *Courtesy of the Collection of William R. & Teresa F. Kurau.*

The Landing Of General Lafayette At Castle Garden, New York, 16 August, 1824 wash pitcher by James & Ralph Clews, 8" high. *Courtesy of the Collection of William R. & Teresa F. Kurau.*

The Landing Of General Lafayette At Castle Garden, New York, 16 August, 1824 creamer by James & Ralph Clews, 4 3/4" high. *Courtesy of the Collection of William R. & Teresa F. Kurau.*

The Landing Of General Lafayette At Castle Garden, New York, 16 August, 1824 creamer by James & Ralph Clews, 8" high. *Courtesy of the Collection of William R. & Teresa F. Kurau.*

The Landing Of General Lafayette At Castle Garden, New York, 16 August, 1824 creamer by James & Ralph Clews, 5 3/8" high. Note here how the print was cut into strips to fit onto the smaller creamers. *Courtesy of the Collection of William R. & Teresa F. Kurau.*

The Landing Of General Lafayette At Castle Garden, New York, 16 August, 1824 sugar bowl by James & Ralph Clews, 6 1/4" high. *Courtesy of the Collection of William R. & Teresa F. Kurau.*

The Landing Of General Lafayette At Castle Garden, New York, 16 August, 1824 soup tureen by James & Ralph Clews, 10 3/4" high. *Courtesy of the Collection of William R. & Teresa F. Kurau.*

The Landing Of General Lafayette At Castle Garden, New York, 16 August, 1824 sauce tureen and undertray by James & Ralph Clews. The tureen measures 6 1/2" x 4" x 5 1/2". *Courtesy of the Collection of William R. & Teresa F. Kurau.*

Peace and Plenty

Suggesting the Roman ideal of the warrior returned to the peaceful farming life, the dark blue printed Peace and Plenty features a toga clad farmer holding a cornucopia or "horn of plenty" and a sickle. He is leaning on a shield with the words "Peace" and "Plenty" stamped on it along with an eagle. A wide band of fruit and flowers decorates the border.

The Landing Of General Lafayette At Castle Garden, New York, 16 August, 1824 creamer by James & Ralph Clews, 4" high. *Courtesy of the Collection of William R. & Teresa F. Kurau.*

Peace And Plenty plate by James & Ralph Clews, 7" in diameter. The title phrase is found of the shield. *Courtesy of Lynn D. Trusdell.*

Peace And Plenty plate by James & Ralph Clews, 8 3/4" in diameter. *Courtesy of the Collection of William R. & Teresa F. Kurau.*

Picturesque Views

The picturesque views combine two subjects: views of Pittsburgh, Pennsylvania and Hudson River views from W.G. Wall's Hudson River Portfolio. These were printed in light blue, purple, pink, brown and black and bordered with flowers, birds and scrolls. The views included:
Bakers Falls, Hudson River; Fairmount (so called); Fort Edward, Hudson River; Fort Montgomery, Hudson River; From Fishkill, Hudson River; Glenn's Falls; Hadley's Falls; Hudson, Hudson River; Jessup's Landing, Hudson River; Junction Of The Sacandaga and Hudson Rivers; Little Falls At Luzerne, Hudson River; Near Fishkill, Hudson River; Near Fort Miller, Hudson River; Near Hudson, Hudson River; Near Sandy Hill, Hudson River; Newburgh, Hudson River; New York, Hudson River; Penitentiary In Allegheny, Near Pittsburgh, Pennsylvania; Pittsburgh-Steamboat Pennsylvania; Pittsburgh-Steamboats Home, Lark & Nile; Rapids Above Hadley's Falls; Troy From Mount Ida; West Point, Hudson River.

Fairmount (so called) cup plate by James & Ralph Clews in light blue and brown, 4 1/8" in diameter. *Courtesy of the Collection of William R. & Teresa F. Kurau.*

The romantic title mark used for the Picturesque Views series featuring both the series name and the title of the individual print. *Courtesy of the Collection of William R. & Teresa F. Kurau.*

Little Falls At Luzerne, Hudson River footed soup tureen by James & Ralph Clews, 13" x 11" 10 1/2" high. *Courtesy of the Collection of William R. & Teresa F. Kurau.*

Near Hudson, Hudson River platter by James & Ralph Clews, 9 3/4" x 8". *Courtesy of the Collection of William R. & Teresa F. Kurau.*

Near Jessup's Landing, Hudson River plate by James & Ralph Clews, 10 1/4" in diameter. *Courtesy of the Collection of William R. & Teresa F. Kurau.*

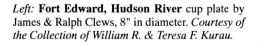

Above right, right: **Near Sandy Hill, Hudson River** cup plates by James & Ralph Clews printed in red and black, 4 3/4" in diameter. *Courtesy of the Collection of William R. & Teresa F. Kurau.*

Left: **Fort Edward, Hudson River** cup plate by James & Ralph Clews, 8" in diameter. *Courtesy of the Collection of William R. & Teresa F. Kurau.*

New York, Hudson River by James & Ralph Clews, 22" x 18 3/4".
Courtesy of the Collection of William R. & Teresa F. Kurau.

West Point, Hudson River plate by James & Ralph Clews, 8" in diameter. *Courtesy of the Collection of William R. & Teresa F. Kurau.*

New York, Hudson River by James & Ralph Clews, 21 3/4" x 17 1/2".
Courtesy of the Collection of William R. & Teresa F. Kurau.

Pittsburgh (Steamboat), Pennsylvania plate by James & Ralph Clews, 10 1/2" in diameter. *Courtesy of the Collection of William R. & Teresa F. Kurau.*

New York, Hudson River well-and-tree platter by James & Ralph Clews, 21 3/4" x 17 1/2". *Courtesy of the Collection of William R. & Teresa F. Kurau.*

Troy From Mount Ida plate by James & Ralph Clews, 10 1/2" in diameter. *Courtesy of the Collection of William R. & Teresa F. Kurau.*

Pittsfield Elm

A winter view of Pittsfield, Massachusetts in dark blue with medallions and flowers decorating the border.

A Winter View Of Pittsfield, Mass. plate by James & Ralph Clews, 10 1/2" in diameter. According to R.T. Haines Halsey this is a very popular series of platters, plates and vegetable dishes. The central building is the First Congregational Church (1793-1853), the right hand structure was the Town Hall, the far left structure was the Berkshire Hotel (1826-1866). The prominent elm was well known for it's size and beauty; the fence erected to protect it was built in 1820. Despite the towns-folk's best efforts, the tree was struck by lightning and torn down in 1861. *Courtesy of the Collection of William R. & Teresa F. Kurau.*

Printed back mark with the title and both the printed manufacturer's name "CLEWS" and the impressed circular crown mark. Both were in use throughout the firms career from c. 1818-1834. *Courtesy of the Collection of William R. & Teresa F. Kurau.*

Thomas Godwin

From 1809 to 1834 Thomas and Benjamin Godwin operated the New Wharf and New Basin potteries, producing creamwares and earthenwares. From 1834 to 1854 Thomas Godwin worked alone, producing transfer printed wares. With the increasing diversity in colors available for transfer printing, Godwin's export trade with America rose and the quality of his wares improved over the years.[20]

Series and Views

American Views

American scenes taken from the views of the United States and Canada produced by W. H. Bartlett. These were printed in light blue, pink, purple and brown and were surrounded by borders of morning glories, moss and leaves or a variation on that theme. These views include: Baltimore; Boston and Bunker Hill; Brooklyn Ferry; Caldwell, Lake George; Columbia Bridge (On The Susquehanna); East Port And Passamaquoddy Bay; Outlet of Lake Memphremagog; Schuylkill Water Works; The Capitol, Washington; The Narrows From Fort Hamilton; The President's House; Utica, N.Y.; Village of Cedars, St. Lawrence; and Yale College.

Marks

Thomas Godwin used a variety of impressed or printed marks including a "T. G." initial mark, several marks with the name of the firm, the town and/or the body material. The printed mark present on the back of The Capitol, Washington plate reads OPAQUE CHINA, T GODWIN, WHARF (for New Wharf) and features a less-than-majestic British lion in the coat of arms.[21]

Thomas Green

Thomas Green produced transfer printed patterns in a variety of colors from the Minerva Works in Fenton, Staffordshire from 1847 to 1859. Color transfers included blue, black, brown, green and pink.[22]

Series and Views

Thomas Green exported a series titled W. Penn's Treaty. A variety of scenes depicting the signing of the 1683 peace treaty between William Penn and North American Indians. The foliage and architecture in these scenes is truly extraordinary for North America.

The Capitol, Washington plate by Thomas Godwin, 10 1/2" in diameter. *Courtesy of the Collection of William R. & Teresa F. Kurau.*

William Penn's Treaty plate by Thomas Green, 7 3/8" in diameter. Note the extraordinary architecture in the background. *Courtesy of the Collection of William R. & Teresa F. Kurau.*

Printed mark with the name of the view and Thomas Green's "T.G." manufacturer's mark which was in use from 1847-1859. *Courtesy of the Collection of William R. & Teresa F. Kurau.*

Marks

Thomas Green used a variety of printed marks including the simple "T. G." shown here. These initials may cause some confusion when distinguishing between Thomas Green and Thomas Godwin above. Other marks include "T. GREEN, FENTON POTTERIES" and "T. G., FENTON" within a Staffordshire knot beneath a crown.[23]

Hall & Son

Ralph Hall produced transfer printed earthenwares for the export market in America from 1822 to 1849 at Swan Bank, Tunstall, Staffordshire. In c. 1836 the company name was changed to Ralph Hall & Son. This did not last long apparently. The wares presented here are enigmatically signed Ric'd Hall & Son. In 1841 the name changed again, this time to Ralph Hall & Company.[24]

Series and Views

Two views produced for the American market include the commemorative **Fayette, The Nations Guest** and is dated to General Lafayette's 1824 return trip to America. The print also features George Washington and the interesting inscription "REPUBLICANS ARE NOT ALWAYS UNGRATEFUL". Beneath this slogan is the signature Ric'd Hall & Son.

The second print is an imaginative patriotic image of the American eagle. This eagle is clasping not only the usual materials in it's claws (flag, battle ax, arrows) but also a sea shell on which the bird appears to be riding over the water in front of an imaginative city scape full of romantic generic architecture.

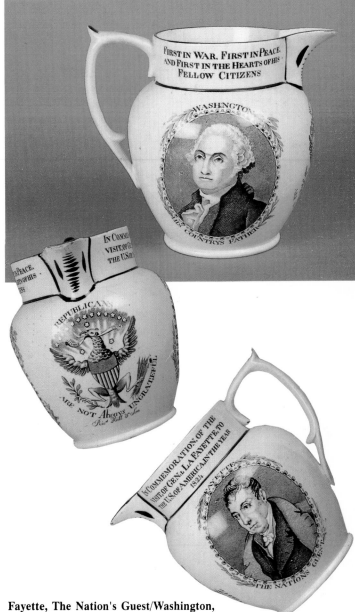

Fayette, The Nation's Guest/Washington, His Country's Father commemorative pitchers in blue and black signed Ric'd Hall & Son, 6 3/4" high each. Interesting in some of it's inscriptions and in the signature of the firm incorporated into the design. *Courtesy of the Collection of William R. & Teresa F. Kurau.*

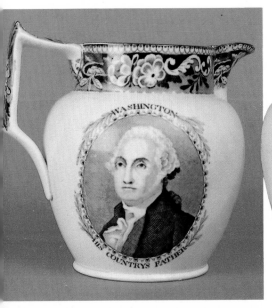

Marks

Ralph Hall employed several printed marks over the years. R. Hall is the constant among them. In c. 1836 the company mark changed from "R. HALL" to "R. HALL & SON." From 1841-1849 the mark changed again, this time to "R. HALL & CO." or "R H & CO."[25]

Ralph Hammersley

Between 1860 and 1905 Ralph Hammersley manufactured earthenwares at several potteries. From 1860 to 1883 Hammersley operated out of the Church Bank Pottery, Tunstall. From 1884 to 1905 the firm operated as Ralph Hammersley & Son.[26]

Series and Views

Ralph Hammersley produced a simple printed American eagle and shield christened **Gem** in both blue and brown. The blue is frequently found as a flowing color. The registration mark accompanying the manufacturer's mark indicates the date of registry was April 23, 1868. This indicates the pattern was produced at the Church Bank Pottery works at Tunstall.

Printed "R. Hammersley" manufacturer's mark with Gem pattern name and registration mark. *Courtesy of the Collection of William R. & Teresa F. Kurau.*

Joseph Heath & Company

Joseph Heath & Company operated out of the Newfield Pottery, Tunstall, Staffordshire from 1828 to 1841 producing a variety of earthenwares. Transfer printed colors tend toward the lighter shades and include a light blue, brown, purple, pink and black. The Romantic Movement influenced the Heath designs.[28]

Series and Views

Joseph Heath & Company produced the view **The Residence of the Late Richard Jordan, New Jersey.** The view features the Quaker minister's home and is bordered either with flowers or a double line.

Gem plate by Ralph Hammersley, 8 3/4" in diameter. Note the simplicity of this later transfer print registered on April 23, 1868 as compared with prints produced in the 1820s and 1830s. *Courtesy of the Collection of William R. & Teresa F. Kurau.*

The Residence of the Late Richard Jordan, New Jersey coffee pot displaying the quaker minister's home by Joseph Heath & Company, 10 1/2" high. *Courtesy of the Collection of William R. & Teresa F. Kurau.*

Marks

The printed name of the firm or the initials "R.H." are found from 1860-1883. The pattern name frequently accompanies the firm's name. From 1884-1905 the mark became "R. H. & S.".[27]

Marks

Joseph Heath used several different printed marks over the years. These included "J. HEATH & CO.", "J. H. & CO.", and the initial J is frequently printed as an I to create a "I. H. & CO." mark.[29]

Henshall, Williamson & Company

This was one of the smaller firms operating out of Longport, Staffordshire. It went through several partnerships including Henshall & Company (c. 1795), Henshall, Williamson & Clowes (c. 1790-1795) and Henshall, Williamson & Company (c. 1802-1828). Much of the confusion originates in the habit of this small firm (common to many of it's limited size and stature) not to mark their wares. The recorded marks to date are for Henshall & Company. The firm produced dark and medium blue transfer prints for the American and the English and European markets. The wares produced were quality products.[30]

Series and Views

Fruit and Flower Border Series

A fruit and flower border surrounds the views in this series. The views were produced of American scenes and buildings. English and European views also employed this border. American views included:
Court House, Baltimore; Exchange, Baltimore; Holliday Street Theater, Baltimore; The Dam and Water Works, Philadelphia (printed with either a side-wheel and stern-wheel steam ship); an unidentified two story structure with two apparently central chimney stacks; Vevay, Indiana(?); and York Minster.

One of two printed back marks used for the Fruit and Flower Border series with the name of each view. The other mark is more oval in shape and composed of thistles on the left and flowers on the right. *Courtesy of the Collection of William R. & Teresa F. Kurau.*

The Dam And Water Works, Philadelphia plate by Henshall, Williamson & Company featuring a central side-wheel steamboat in the foreground, 10" in diameter. *Courtesy of the Collection of William R. & Teresa F. Kurau.*

The Dam And Water Works, Philadelphia plate with a central stern-wheel steamboat in the foreground by Henshall, Williamson & Company, 10" in diameter. *Courtesy of the Collection of William R. & Teresa F. Kurau.*

Court House, Baltimore plate by Henshall, Williamson & Company, 8 3/4" in diameter. *Courtesy of the Collection of William R. & Teresa F. Kurau.*

Unidentified building cup plate by Henshall, Williamson & Company, 3 1/2" in diameter. *Courtesy of the Collection of William R. & Teresa F. Kurau.*

Vevay, Indiana plates by Henshall, Williamson & Company, 6" and 6 5/ 8" in diameter. *Courtesy of the Collection of William R. & Teresa F. Kurau.*

Marks

Henshall, Williamson & Company apparently felt little need to mark their wares. The only recorded mark to date is for the c. 1795 Henshall & Company and is simply the name of the firm impressed "HENSHALL & CO."[31]

Job & John Jackson

Job and John Jackson produced earthenwares from the Church Yard Works, Burslem, Staffordshire from 1831 to 1835. The Jacksons produced transfer printed wares in light blue, purple, sepia, pink and black. Their borders were open and flowered in a manner typical for this period. Their wares were largely targeted to the American export trade.[32]

Series and Views

Much of Job & John Jackson's production was destined for America and featured American views. These were grouped generally under American Scenery and Skenectady on the Mohawk River. The Skenectady view features a central view of Skenectady, New York originally produced by W. G. Wall, and several miscellaneous views.

Job & John Jackson simply used the name of the view and their manufacturer's mark to identify their wares. Unlike some Staffordshire potters, no special mark was produced for each series by this firm. *Courtesy of the Collection of William R. & Teresa F. Kurau.*

American Scenery

The views of scenery and architecture from various regions of the United States were produced in light blue, pink, purple, green, brown, and black and bordered with long stemmed roses. These included:
Albany, New York; American Scenery ... View of Newburgh; American Scenery ... Conway, New Hampshire; At Richmond, Virginia; Battery & C, New York; B a t t l e Monument, Baltimore; Bunker Hill Monument; C i t y Hall, New York; Deaf & Dumb Asylum, Philadelphia; Fort Conanicut, Rhode Island; Fort Ticonderoga, New York; Girard's Bank, Philadelphia; Hancock House, Boston; Hartford, Connecticut; Harvard Hall, Mass.; I r o n Works at Saugerties; Lake George; New Haven, Connecticut; Newport, Rhode Island; Shannondale Springs, Virginia; Skenectady On the Mohawk River; State House, Boston; The President's House, Washington; The Race Bridge, Philadelphia; The Water Works, Philadelphia; University Hall, Harvard; Upper Ferry Bridge Over the River Schuylkill; View of the Canal, Little Falls, Mohawk River; View of the Catskill Mountain House, N.Y.; View of Newburgh; Yale College; and State House, New Haven.

Battery & C, New York plate by Job & John Jackson, 7 7/8" in diameter. *Courtesy of the Collection of William R. & Teresa F. Kurau.*

Battle Monument, Baltimore plate by Job & John Jackson, 9" in diameter. *Courtesy of the Collection of William R. & Teresa F. Kurau.*

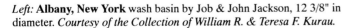

Left: **Albany, New York** wash basin by Job & John Jackson, 12 3/8" in diameter. *Courtesy of the Collection of William R. & Teresa F. Kurau.*

Hartford, Connecticut plates in brown and black by Job & John Jackson, each measuring 10 1/4" in diameter. *Courtesy of the Collection of William R. & Teresa F. Kurau.*

New Haven, Connecticut platter by Job & John Jackson, 10 5/8" x 8 7/8". *Courtesy of the Collection of William R. & Teresa F. Kurau.*

The President's House, Washington plate by Job & John Jackson, 10 3/8" in diameter. *Courtesy of the Collection of William R. & Teresa F. Kurau.*

View of Newburgh potato bowl by Job & John Jackson, 11" in diameter. *Courtesy of the Collection of William R. & Teresa F. Kurau.*

Skenectady on the Mohawk River

This view is bordered in peacock feathers and flowers and was printed in pink, purple and black.

Skenectady On The Mohawk River pitcher by Job & John Jackson, 8" high. *Courtesy of the Collection of William R. & Teresa F. Kurau.*

Albany platter by Charles Meigh, 13 1/2" x 10 1/4". *Courtesy of the Collection of William R. & Teresa F. Kurau.*

Utica plate by Charles Meigh, 7 1/4" in diameter. *Courtesy of the Collection of William R. & Teresa F. Kurau.*

Charles Meigh from 1835-1849 created many impressed marks featuring his full name. The majority of Charles Meigh's printed marks used the initials "C. M." with the pattern name and body type. Many marks included the Royal Arms.[40]

When Charles Meigh's son Charles joined the firm in 1851 the initials on the variety of printed marks employed were changed to "C. M. & S." or "M. & S." This would continue until 1861. Pattern names and body types were frequently included. The Royal Arms were incorporated into several marks.[41]

Printed back mark used for the American Cities and Scenery series featuring the series name within a rock, the name of the view beneath it and the initials "C. M." manufacturer's mark. The initials of the manufacturer were used in most printed marks by Charles Meigh from 1835-1849. *Courtesy of the Collection of William R. & Teresa F. Kurau.*

Marks

Job Meigh used an impressed name mark "MEIGH" from 1805-1834, an impressed or printed "OLD HALL" mark in 1805 and the initials "J. M. & S." when his son Charles joined him in c. 1812. This mark was used, at times in conjunction with a printed design until 1834.[39]

Mellor, Venables & Company

Mellor, Venables & Company produced earthenwares and china from the Hole House Pottery, Burslem, Staffordshire from 1834 to 1851. The company produced a variety of transfer printed earthenwares for the American market. American scenes and arms of the American states were produced.[42]

Series and Views

Arms of the States

These contain the seals of eight American states Delaware, Maryland, Massachusetts, Mississippi, New York, North Carolina, Pennsylvania, and Virginia. These are surrounded by a border featuring medallions of the seals of the American states in different combinations.

Arms Of The States polychrome printed teapot by Mellor, Venables & Company, 8 1/2" high. *Courtesy of the Collection of William R. & Teresa F. Kurau.*

Scenic Views—-Arms of the States Border

The scenic views in the center were taken from W. H. Bartlett's views of the United States, printed in dark blue. The borders featured a series of seals of twenty-one American states. The original thirteen and Alabama, Illinois, Indiana, Kentucky, Michigan, Mississippi, Missouri and Ohio. The views themselves included:
Albany; Boston and Bunker Hill; Caldwell (Lake George); The Narrows (From Fort Hamilton); The President's House from the River; The Tomb of Washington, Mount Vernon; View from Gowanus Heights, Brooklyn; View of Balti-more; View of Hudson City and the Catskill Mountains; View of New York from Weehawken; View of the Capitol at Washington; Village of Little Falls (Mohawk River); Washington's House, Mount Vernon.

Marks

The name, either printed out or as the initials "M. V. & CO.", is the standard feature of several impressed or printed marks. The printed pattern name is also frequently included.[43]

Francis Morley & Company

Francis Morley & Company was producing earthenwares, ironstones and other white bodied earthenwares at Broad Street, Shelton, Hanley, Staffordshire from 1845 to 1858. The firm had previously been Ridgway & Morley and would become Morley & Ashworth. The firm acquired the equipment of Charles J. Mason & Company, their engraver, and the rights to use the Mason's Patent Ironstone China name and mark.[44]

Series and Views

The firm produced the American Marine and Lake Series.

American Marine

A number of views of sailing vessels bordered with medallions of additional sailing vessels were printed in blue, red and brown. This pattern was continued by George L. Ashworth and Brother following their purchase of the Morley pottery in 1862. This pattern has resurfaced over the years as G. L. Ashworth Brothers continues today.

Lake Series

The views for this series were taken from W. H. Bartlett's engravings of Canada. They were printed in blue, purple, pink and brown. The central view was surrounded by a border of flowers and scrolls. Difficulties arise from the fact that these views are poorly marked, usually only with the series name Lake and none with the pattern name. Another difficulty is their similarity with patterns by Heath, Podmore, Walker and Company and Wedgwood. The views included:
The Chaudiere Bridge; The Church at Point Levi; Georgeville; Hallowell (Bay of Quinte); Rideau Canal, Bytown; Scene of 1000 Isles; View on the St. Lawrence/ Indian Encampment; and Village of Cedars, River St. Lawrence.

Scene of 1000 Isles plate by Francis Morley & Company, 9 1/4" in diameter. *Courtesy of the Collection of William R. & Teresa F. Kurau.*

Marks

This firm produced a number of impressed and printed marks with the initials "F. M.", "F. M. & CO." or with the full name of the firm "F. MORLEY & CO."[45]

Edward & George Phillips

From 1822 to 1834, Edward & George Phillips manufactured earthenwares in Longport, Staffordshire. The firm produced several blue transfer printed design.[46]

Series and Views

For American export the pattern Franklin featuring the urn ornamented tomb of this Founding Father with two individuals drawing inspiration from the sight. This was a very romantic notion of the period.

Franklin tea cup without a handle by Edward & George Phillips. This view depicts Franklin's tomb with a couple gathering inspiration from a respectful distance. *Courtesy of the Collection of William R. & Teresa F. Kurau.*

Rideau Canal, Bytown plate originally by Francis Morley & Company and produced by the succeeding firm, G. L. Ashworth & Brothers from 1862-1880, 9" in diameter. *Courtesy of the Collection of William R. & Teresa F. Kurau.*

Printed series name mark used for the Lake series and an impressed "ASHWORTH" manufacturer's mark used by G. L. Ashworth Brothers, the successor firm of Francis Morley & Company. Ashworth Brothers was in business from 1862 to 1880. *Courtesy of the Collection of William R. & Teresa F. Kurau.*

Marks

The firm produced a variety of printed marks, frequently including the pattern name. The manufacturer's name was presented in several ways: "PHILLIPS, LONGPORT", "E. & G. P.", "E. & G. PHILLIPS, LONGPORT".[47]

Podmore, Walker & Company

The company began their operations in Tunstall in 1834. The firm continued as Podmore, Walker & Company until 1859. Enoch Wedgwood became a partner in the pottery in c. 1856. Between c. 1856-1859, the firm used the mark "P.W. & W." for Podmore, Walker & Wedgwood. Enoch Wedgwood took over the older establishment in 1859 and changed the name to Wedgwood & Company.[48]

The product of the firm was dinner and toilet sets in earthenware bodies heralded as Pearl Stone Ware and Imperial Ironstone China. The wares were brightly painted, sponged, or decorated with transfer prints.[49]

Series and Views

Podmore, Walker & Company produced a series of views entitled British America which were views from Canada. These were printed in blue, green and black with a border of ferns on moss. The mark for these reads "P. W. & Co., British America." The views in the series included: Kingston, Lake Ontario; Montreal; Navy Island (Niagara River); Quebec; and View on the St. Lawrence/Indian Encampment.

Marks

Podmore, Walker & Company used the initials "P.W. & CO." on several printed and impressed marks from 1834-1859 and frequently included the pattern names. The initials "P.W. & W." were employed from c. 1856-1859 when Enoch Wedgwood joined the firm.[50]

The Ridgway Family

The Ridgway family were Staffordshire potters primarily associated with two Hanley potteries, the Bell Works (1792) and Cauldon Place (1802). Two brothers, Job and George Ridgway, formed a partnership until Job Ridgway built Cauldon Works. Job was joined by his sons John and William Ridgway from c. 1808 to 1814. The wares produced maintained a very high quality and the American views were well received. The Ridgway brother's enjoyed a thriving export business with America.[51]

John and William ran the works from 1814 to 1830, producing historical Staffordshire wares sold to the American export market among others. After 1830, until c. 1855, John directed the Cauldon Place Works while William ran the Bell Works. Cauldon Place Works would pass into the hands of Brown-Westhead, Moore & Company in 1862 and then to Cauldon Ltd. in 1905.[52]

The Ridgway potteries produced useful wares of high workmanship in earthenwares, stonewares, and porcelain. Tea and dessert sets were specialties of the Ridgways. After 1830, William Ridgway manufactured finely molded jugs, stonewares, teapots, and candlesticks as well as delicate and finely decorated porcelain-styled tinted earthenware and stone china.[53]

The Cauldon Place Works ceramics were described by Jewitt as, "... embrac[ing] almost every description of ceramic. In earthenware, all the usual table and toilet services and useful and ornamental articles of every class are made."[54]

Series and Views

American Scenery

Printed back mark used with the American Scenery series featuring the name of the view and William Ridgway's W. R. initial manufacturer's mark in use from c. 1830-1834. The firm, as William Ridgway and Company, was in business from c. 1830-1854. Several examples have an impressed lion and unicorn W. R. & CO. mark. This mark christens William Ridgway's white ware body "OPAQUE GRANITE CHINA". *Courtesy of the Collection of William R. & Teresa F. Kurau.*

Views taken from the book American Scenery featuring Bartlett's work. American scenery was published in 1840. The views were printed in light blue, purple, brown and black. The borders were narrow bands of lace and regularly spaced clusters of three small flowers. Black transfer printed views featured no border. The views included: Albany; Caldwell, Lake George; Columbia Bridge on the Susquehanna; Crow-Nest from Bull Hill; Delaware Water Gap, Pa.; Harper's Ferry from the Potomac Side; Meredith; Narrows from Staten Island; Peekskill Landing, Hudson River; The Narrows from Fort Hamilton; The Valley of the Shenandoah from Jefferson's Rock; Undercliff Near Cold Spring; View of the Capitol at Washington; View from Port Putnam, Hudson River; View from Ruggle's House, Newburgh, Hudson River; Wilkes-Barre, Vale of Wyoming.

Columbia Bridge On The Susquehanna vegetable dish by William Ridgway (& Company), 12 1/8" in length. *Courtesy of the Collection of William R. & Teresa F. Kurau.*

The Valley Of The Shenandoah From Jefferson's Rock cup plate by William Ridgway (& Company), 4 3/4" in diameter. *Courtesy of the Collection of William R. & Teresa F. Kurau.*

Peekskill Landing, Hudson River vegetable dish by William Ridgway (& Company), 10" x 7 1/4" x 2". *Courtesy of the Collection of William R. & Teresa F. Kurau.*

Peekskill Landing, Hudson River vegetable dish by William Ridgway (& Company), 9 3/4" x 7 1/4". *Courtesy of the Collection of William R. & Teresa F. Kurau.*

View From Port Putnam, Hudson River platter by William Ridgway (& Company), 16 3/4" x 12 3/4". *Courtesy of the Collection of William R. & Teresa F. Kurau.*

View from Ruggle's House, Newburgh, Hudson River plate by William Ridgway (& Company), 10 3/8" in diameter. *Courtesy of the Collection of William R. & Teresa F. Kurau.*

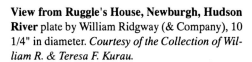

View from Ruggle's House, Newburgh, Hudson River plate by William Ridgway (& Company), 10 1/4" in diameter. *Courtesy of the Collection of William R. & Teresa F. Kurau.*

Beauties of America

Printed back mark used for most of the Beauties of America series, displaying the series name, title of the view and the manufacturer's mark. *Courtesy of the Collection of William R. & Teresa F. Kurau.*

These prints display the architectural beauties of America of the period in dark blue. The prints are bordered by rose medallions. The individual views include: Almshouse, Boston; Almshouse, New York; Athenaeum, Boston; Bank, Savannah; Cambridge College, Massachusetts; Capitol, Washington; City Hall, New York; Court House, Boston; Custom House, Philadelphia; Deaf and Dumb Asylum, Hartford, Con.; Exchange, Baltimore; Exchange, Charleston; Hospital, Boston; Insane Hospital, Boston; Library, Philadelphia; Masonic Hall, Philadelphia; Mount Vernon Near Washington; Octagon Church, Boston; Pennsylvania Hospital, Philadelphia; St. Paul's Church, Boston; Staughton's Church, Philadelphia; State House, Boston.

Almshouse, New York platter by John & William Ridgway, 16 3/4" x 12 3/4". *Courtesy of the Collection of William R. & Teresa F. Kurau.*

Almshouse, Boston large soup tureen (missing it's handle) by John & William Ridgway, 14" high. *Courtesy of the Collection of William R. & Teresa F. Kurau.*

City Hall, New York plate by John & William Ridgway, 9 3/4" in diameter. *Courtesy of the Collection of William R. & Teresa F. Kurau.*

Exchange, Charleston open handled tray by John & William Ridgway, 8 1/4". Note that the exchange has a different printed back mark from most in the Beauties of America series. *Courtesy of the Collection of William R. & Teresa F. Kurau.*

Exchange, Charleston fruit compote by John & William Ridgway, 9 3/4" in diameter, 5 1/4" high. *Courtesy of the Collection of William R. & Teresa F. Kurau.*

Bank, Savannah fruit compote by John & William Ridgway, 9 3/4" in diameter, 5 1/4" high. *Courtesy of the Collection of William R. & Teresa F. Kurau.*

Court House, Boston small footed tray by John & William Ridgway, 10" x 8" x 1 1/2". *Courtesy of the Collection of William R. & Teresa F. Kurau.*

Hospital, Boston vegetable dish by John & William Ridgway, 11 1/4" x 8 1/2" x 2". *Courtesy of the Collection of William R. & Teresa F. Kurau.*

Octagon Church, Boston soup bowl by John & William Ridgway, 9 3/4" in diameter. *Courtesy of the Collection of William R. & Teresa F. Kurau.*

St. Paul's Church, Boston platter by John & William Ridgway, 9 3/8" x 6 5/8". *Courtesy of the Collection of William R. & Teresa F. Kurau.*

Catskill Moss

Printed back mark used for Catskill Moss series includes the series name and the name of each view. These also have registration marks which are very helpful in dating the initial registration date of the design. In this case the design was registered December 16, 1844. From the registration records, the enigmatic C.C. was traced to William Ridgway, Son & Company of Hanley (c. 1841-1846). *Courtesy of the Collection of William R. & Teresa F. Kurau.*

Bartlett's views in American Scenery were used again in these transfer prints. They were printed in light blue and the central views were surrounded with a border of clusters of moss over a regular background of moss. The views included:

Anthony's Nose; Baltimore; Boston and Bunker's Hill; Caldwell, Lake George; Centre Harbour; Columbia Bridge on the Susquehanna; East Port; Fairmount; Fairmount Gardens; Hudson, New York; Kosciusko's Tomb; Little Falls, N.Y.; Meredith; Near Troy, N.Y.; Near Weehawken; New York Bay (Brooklyn from Gowanus Heights); President's House; Saw-Mill at Centre Harbour; The Narrows from Fort Hamilton; The Narrows, Lake George; Undercliff Near Cold Spring; Utica; Valley of Wyoming; Village of Catskill; Washington's Tomb; Wilkes-Barre, Vale of Wyoming.

Near Weehawken wash pitcher (part of a chamber set) by William Ridgway, Sons & Company, 11" high. *Courtesy of the Collection of William R. & Teresa F. Kurau.*

Near Weehawken view is printed on the exterior of this footbath and **Boston And Bunker's Hill** (virtually identical to a view by the same name in the American Views by Thomas Godwin) adorns the inside. Footbaths were manufactured by many nineteenth century potters and used to soak tired feet in mustard baths. Before 1830 the sides of footbaths were vertical, afterwards they took on the curved form seen here. This footbath was produced by William Ridgway, Sons & Company and measures 8 1/2" x 19" x 13". *Courtesy of the Collection of William R. & Teresa F. Kurau.*

Utica vegetable bowl by William Ridgway, Sons & Company, 11" x 8 3/4" x 2 1/4". *Courtesy of the Collection of William R. & Teresa F. Kurau.*

Wilkes-Barre, Vale Of Wyoming sugar bowl by William Ridgway, Sons & Company, 5" in diameter, 8" hi h. *Courtesy of the Collection of William R. & Teresa F. Kurau.*

Columbian Star, Oct. 28th, 1840

Printed back mark featuring the series name, date and the manufacturer's name, John Ridgway, who produced earthenwares from Cauldon Place from c. 1830-1855. *Courtesy of the Collection of William R. & Teresa F. Kurau.*

The center view is a log cabin used by the William Henry Harrison presidential campaign of 1840. What early candidate did not want to be associated with such humble origins. This print was produced in light blue, green, pink, brown and black with a border of large stars against a background of smaller stars. Three views were produced: the log cabin seen from an end view with two men, the same cabin from a three-quarters view, and the cabin three-quarters view with a man plowing a field with a two horse team in the foreground.

Two views of the log cabin used as a symbol of the candidacy of William Henry Harrison. As many have done before and since, this campaign was run without any real issues. The campaign relied entirely on emphasizing Harrison's link with the common man (hence the log cabin) and his military career. The sugar bowl (left) is adorned with **Log Cabin** (side view) and the plate is decorated with **Log Cabin** (side view, man plowing with a two horse team). These were produced by John Ridgway. The sugar bowl measures 6 x 6" and the plate measures 9" in diameter. *Courtesy of the Collection of William R. & Teresa F. Kurau.*

Marks

The Ridgway family used a number of printed and impressed marks of varying designs. One regular feature was the presence of the family name or initials in the marks.

From 1814 to 1830 the name or initials of John & William Ridgway were used as "J. W. R.", "J. & W. R." or "J. & W. Ridgway". These were often included with the pattern name.

From c. 1830-1854, William Ridgway used his name "W. RIDGWAY" or initials with a variety of mark designs. In c. 1841 his son joined him and the name became "W. RIDGWAY, SON & CO." on the marks.[55]

"J. & W. RIDGWAY" printed manufacturer's mark of John & William Ridgway in use from c. 1814-1830. *Courtesy of the Collection of William R. & Teresa F. Kurau.*

William Ridgway's W. R. initial manufacturer's mark in use from c. 1830-1834 and the impressed lion and unicorn mark of William Ridgway and Company, which was in business from c. 1830-1854. The lion and unicorn features the initials "W. R. & CO." and the name they gave their version of white ware, "OPAQUE GRANITE CHINA". *Courtesy of the Collection of William R. & Teresa F. Kurau.*

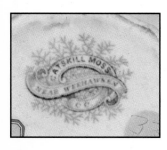

The enigmatic C.C. on this mark has been traced through the registration records to William Ridgway, Son & Company of Hanley. The firm was in business from c. 1841-1846. *Courtesy of the Collection of William R. & Teresa F. Kurau.*

Series and Views

Boston Harbor

Printed in a dark blue, the central image is the American eagle with shield and wings spread in the foreground. The city of Boston is set off in the distance. The border is composed of flowers, foliage and scroll work.

John Rogers & Son

John Rogers and his son Spencer produced good quality earthenwares at Dale Hall, Longport, Staffordshire from circa 1814 to 1836 when the pottery closed. The firms produced large amounts of ceramics in a range of patterns and shapes. These were manufactured largely for the English market. Unlike most Staffordshire potters producing for the American export market, Rogers & Son limited themselves only to a few special patterns. The most noteworthy was the Boston State House print which carried a great deal of significance for Americans during the period. Rogers & Son produced three different engravings of Boston's state house including nearly identical to a print by Stubbs. Depicted in the foreground are cows and sheep. It makes you wonder what the fellow with the wheelbarrow is transporting. In the 1840s, Charles Dickens visited the state house and remarked on the beauty of the surroundings. Dickens made no mention of either sheep or cows.[56]

Boston State House

John Rogers & Son printed mark featuring American eagle with wings spread in a simplified version of the Great Seal. *Courtesy of the Collection of William R. & Teresa F. Kurau.*

The view presented was from the Boston Common toward the state house and dated from 1804. The border was composed of flowers and leaves and the print was produced in dark blue.

Boston State House platter by John Rogers & Son, 14 3/4" x 11 1/4". *Courtesy of the Collection of William R. & Teresa F. Kurau.*

Boston State House charger by John Rogers & Son, 16 3/4" in diameter with a 2" lip. *Courtesy of the Collection of William R. & Teresa F. Kurau.*

Boston State House small wash pitcher & basin by John Rogers & Son. The pitcher measures 7 1/4" in diameter and the bowl measures 4 3/4" high and 12" in diameter. *Courtesy of the Collection of William R. & Teresa F. Kurau.*

Shells and Seaweed

More likely to have appealed to Canadians than to the consumers in the United States, the central views (there are five) feature some aspect of the defeat of the Frigate Lapique by the Frigate HMS Blanche. The views tell the story of the battle. These were printed in a medium blue and bordered with shells and seaweed.

Marks

Rogers & Son used the impressed mark "ROGERS" which had previously been used by J. & G. Rogers. This mark was in use from circa 1784 to 1836. Geoffrey Godden states that many well potted blue printed wares bear this mark, most from the years 1800 to 1820.[57]

The impressed "ROGERS" manufacturer's mark was used by John Rogers & Son from c. 1814-1836. It should be noted, however, that this impressed mark was also used by the predecessor of this firm, John & George Rogers, from c. 1784-1814. *Courtesy of the Collection of William R. & Teresa F. Kurau.*

Anthony Shaw

Anthony Shaw produced earthenwares in the Staffordshire potting town of Tunstall from circa 1851 to 1856 and from Burslem from circa 1860 to 1900. For the American export market Shaw produced a series of views from the 1846-1848 war with Mexico sparked by the breakdown of negotiations between the United States and Mexico over the purchase of New Mexico. American troops move into the disputed territory, defeating the Mexican troops at Palo Alto. The United States at that point declared war, moves into Santa Fe and annexes New Mexico. All of this occurred in five months from April of 1846 to August. In 1847 American forces captured Mexico city and in February of 1848 the Treaty of Guadalupe Hidalgo ended the war. The United States gained Texas, New Mexico, California, Utah, Nevada, Arizona, and portions of Colorado and Wyoming in the process.[58]

Series and Views

Texian Campaigne

Scenes from the war, the total number of scenes is unclear, were printed in blue, purple, brown and black. These included:
the Battle of Buena Vista; the Battle of Monterey; the Battle of Palo Alto; the Battle of Resaca de la Palma; the Battle of Chapultepec; a General on a rearing horse, commanding his officers toward the distant battle; and Officers and men at rest around the fire.

Texian Campaigne platter depicting a pitched battle by a bridge by Anthony Shaw, 11" x 9". *Courtesy of the Collection of William R. & Teresa F. Kurau.*

Marks

Shaw employed several impressed and printed marks. The common feature, the firm's name, appeared in it's entirety, as "A. SHAW" or "SHAWS". Added to the mark was "& SON" from circa 1882 to circa 1898. This was altered to "& CO." from circa 1898 until the firm was purchased by A. J. Wilkinson Ltd. in about 1900.[59]

Andrew Stevenson

Andrew Stevenson produced vast supplies of dark blue printed earthenwares in Cobridge, Staffordshire between 1816 and 1830. Prior to 1816, Andrew Stevenson had been involved in the partnership of Bucknall and Stevenson. During his years as an independent potter, Stevenson enjoyed a thriving export trade with America. He used portrait medallion borders emblazoned with the likenesses of Washington, Lafayette, Jefferson and Clinton to good effect. His brother Ralph Stevenson (circa 1810-1832) would do the same. The majority of the sixteen American views credited to Andrew Stevenson were taken from the Hudson River Port Folio works of W. G. Wall, the Irish artist from Dublin who toured America around 1818 and produced sketches of some of the more significant edifices in New York. Among these noteworthy structures were the Almshouse, City Hall and the Catholic Cathedral.[60]

Andrew Stevenson also manufactured series of English views of country houses and castles. These were also exported to America, some with medallion portraits of George Washington and DeWitt Clinton. Most, however, sported borders of roses and other flowers.[61]

Series and Views

Floral Border Series

Printed mark used throughout the Floral Border series, bearing the name of the view and attributing the original art work to W. G. Wall, the Irish artist who visited America c. 1818. *Courtesy of the Collection of William R. & Teresa F. Kurau.*

This series presented three of W. G. Wall's New York views in dark blue transfer prints surrounded by a mixed floral and leaf border. The views are:
New York From Brooklyn Heights; View of Governor's Island; and View on the Road to Lake George.

View Of Governor's Island printed on a large soup bowl by Andrew Stevenson, 10 1/4" in diameter. *Courtesy of the Collection of William R. & Teresa F. Kurau.*

Floral and Scroll Border Series

New York From Brooklyn Heights plate by Andrew Stevenson, 10 1/4" in diameter. *Courtesy of the Collection of William R. & Teresa F. Kurau.*

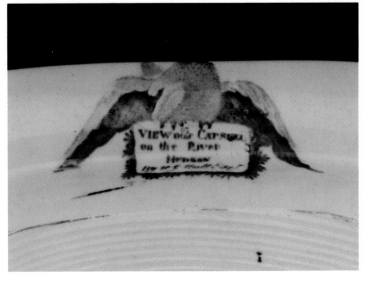

Three printed back marks found on the Floral and Scroll Border series including the name of the view. The eagle marks feature the W. G. Wall attribution. Note the clear, circular, impressed A. Stevenson manufacturer's mark (used from c. 1816-1830) overlapped by the printed urn mark. *Courtesy of the Collection of William R. & Teresa F. Kurau.*

This was a more extensive series of New York views and also included the Perry temple of fame. These were also printed in dark blue. The views were surrounded with a border of flowers interspersed with scrolls. This series included views of the:

Almshouse, New York; Catholic Cathedral, New York; Church and Buildings Adjoining Murray Street, New York; City Hall, New York; Columbia College, New York; New York From Heights Near Brooklyn; The Junction of the Sacandaga and Hudson Rivers; The Temple of Fame...To the Memory of Commodore Perry;   Troy from Mt. Ida; View Near Catskill on the River Hudson; View of New York From Weehawk; and a view of Edinburgh, Scotland marked W. G. Wall.

New York From Heights Near Brooklyn platter by Andrew Stevenson measuring 16 1/2" x 12 3/4". *Courtesy of the Collection of William R. &*

Catholic Cathedral, New York plate by Andrew Stevenson, 6 1/2" in diameter. *Courtesy of the Collection of William R. & Teresa F. Kurau.*

New York From Weehawk platter by Andrew Stevenson measuring 18 1/2" x 14 1/2". *Courtesy of the Collection of William R. & Teresa F. Kurau.*

View Near Catskills On The River Hudson platter by Andrew Stevenson, 12 1/2" x 10 3/4". *Courtesy of the Collection of William R. & Teresa F. Kurau.*

Lafayette

Printed in blue, black or in rust red with a polychrome or blue border, the general facing left or right; these printed testimonials all bore the following inscription at the very least: "General La Fayette. Welcome to the Land of Liberty. He was born at Auvergne in France 1757, joined the American struggle in 1777, and in 1824 returned to repose in the bosom of the land whose liberty he in part gave birth to." The border is comprised of a raised floral motif of enamel and/or lustre decorations. Other border options include an embossed floral motif bracketed by a blue band on either side, and a printed vine leaf border.

General La Fayette, Welcome To The Land Of Liberty commemorative pitcher with a longer biography of the general by Andrew Stevenson. *Courtesy of the Collection of William R. & Teresa F. Kurau.*

General La Fayette, Welcome To The Land Of Liberty commemorative plate issued for Lafayette's return to American shores in 1824 by Andrew Stevenson, 7.5" in diameter. *Courtesy of the Collection of William R. & Teresa F. Kurau.*

Miscellaneous views

These printed views include the Dutch Church at Albany and Wadsworth Tower — complete with a border strikingly similar to the irregular center shell border of Enoch Wood.

Marks

Andrew Stevenson employed a variety of predominantly impressed marks. Difficulty in identification occurs when the name on the mark is simply "STEVENSON" as this could be attributable to either Andrew or his brother Ralph. Other impressed Andrew Stevenson marks include the name "A. STEVENSON" and "Stevenson" impressed in an arc over a three masted sailing ship.[62]

Andrew Stevenson impressed manufacturer's mark. A circular mark with a central crown and around the surface of the circle "A. STEVENSON WARRANTED STAFFORDSHIRE". This mark was in use from c. 1816-1830. *Courtesy of the Collection of William R. & Teresa F. Kurau.*

Impressed STEVENSON manufacturer's mark which may be a source of confusion since both brothers Andrew and Ralph used this mark from c. 1816-1830. *Courtesy of the Collection of William R. & Teresa F. Kurau.*

Ralph Stevenson/Ralph Stevenson & Williams

Ralph Stevenson began manufacturing well crafted and decorated earthenware on his own in Cobridge earlier than his brother Andrew. Ralph Stevenson produced his wares at the Lower Manufactory in Cobridge, Staffordshire from roughly 1810 to 1835. Around 1825, Ralph formed the short-lived partnership Ralph Stevenson & Williams. In 1832 Ralph was joined by his son. The pottery continued as Ralph Stevenson & Son until 1835.[63]

Transfer printed wares decorated the majority of the earthenwares produced by Ralph Stevenson. This included a variety of prints specifically designed for the American export market. In fact, Ralph Stevenson enjoyed a brisk export trade to American shores, as did his brother Andrew. An acorn and oak leaf border series was produced both for American and British consumption, each featuring different views.[64]

Ralph and Andrew Stevenson, along with Ralph Stevenson & Williams, produced a series of views with medallion borders featuring the images of George Washington, General Lafayette, Thomas Jefferson, and DeWitt Clinton. Smaller grouping with from one to three medallions were also printed. One problem with both of the Stevenson's printed wares, many are merely marked "STEVENSON" and deciding which Stevenson produced what becomes tricky.[65]

Ralph Stevenson also produced English views of Dorney Court and Windsor Castle for American consumption. These included small vignettes of the Erie Canal and medallions of Washington, Lafayette, Jefferson and Clinton.[66]

Series and Views

Acorn and Oak Leaves Border Series

Printed back marks used throughout the Acorn & Oak Leaves Border series, with and without the manufacturer's, Ralph Stevenson & William (c. 1825), initials. This was an apparently short-lived partnership between Ralph Stevenson and Aldborough Lloyd Williams. *Courtesy of the Collection of William R. & Teresa F. Kurau.*

American architecture and medallion portraits are the central subjects of this series. These were printed in dark blue and surrounded with an acorns and oak leaves border. English views with this border were printed on hollow wares and platters. The American views included:
Albany Theatre, 1824; A View of the Late Protestant Dutch Church in the City of Albany ... Erected in 1715 ... Pulled Down in 1806; Baltimore Exchange, City Hotel, New York; Columbia College, New York; Harvard College — four structures; Harvard College —- University Hall with a horseman in the foreground; Harvard College — University Hall end view with two people in foreground; Nahant Hotel Near Boston; Octagon Church, Boston; Park Theatre, New York; President Washington; St. Paul's Chapel, New York; State House, Boston; Staughton's Church, Philadelphia; Scudder's American Museum; and Water Works, Philadelphia.

City Hotel, New York plate by Ralph Stevenson & Williams, 8 1/2" in diameter. *Courtesy of the Collection of William R. & Teresa F. Kurau.*

St. Paul's Chapel, New York plate by Ralph Stevenson & William, 6 1/4" in diameter. *Courtesy of the Collection of William R. & Teresa F. Kurau.*

Court House, Boston by Ralph Stevenson & Williams, 5 1/4" in diameter. *Courtesy of the Collection of William R. & Teresa F. Kurau.*

Left: **Columbia College, New York** plate by Ralph Stevenson & Williams, 7 1/2" in diameter. *Courtesy of the Collection of William R. & Teresa F. Kurau.*

Park Theatre, New York plate by Ralph Stevenson & Williams, 9 3/4" in diameter. *Courtesy of the Collection of William R. & Teresa F. Kurau.*

Scudder's American Museum plate by Ralph Stevenson & Williams measuring 7 1/4" in diameter. *Courtesy of the Collection of William R. & Teresa F. Kurau.*

State House, Boston cup plate by Ralph Stevenson & Williams, 4 7/8" in diameter. *Courtesy of the Collection of William R. & Teresa F. Kurau.*

Scudder's American Museum 4 3/4" diameter cup plate by Ralph Stevenson & Williams. *Courtesy of the Collection of William R. & Teresa F. Kurau.*

Water Works, Philadelphia plate by Ralph Stevenson & Williams, 10" in diameter. The Conestoga wagon in the foreground, designed in the Conestoga Valley of Lancaster County, Pennsylvania, was used to deliver army supplies in the War of 1812 and to move migrating Americans into the Midwest and further. A heavy hauler, the Conestoga could move up to 10 tons with six or ten horse teams. The driver frequently sat on the left-hand wheel horse as seen here. *Courtesy of the Collection of William R. & Teresa F. Kurau.*

Lace Border

Printed back mark used for the Lace Border series and containing both the name of the view, the name of the border and the manufacturer's initials "R. S.". *Courtesy of the Collection of William R. & Teresa F. Kurau.*

American towns and transportation centers depicted by Captain Basil Hall during his 1827-1828 American tour provide the central views for this series. The prints were produced in purple, pink, brown and black. The border featured floral sprays over a lace background. The views include:

the Erie Canal at Buffalo; New Orleans; Riceborough, Georgia; and a Shipping Port on the Ohio, Kentucky.

City Hall, Albany, plate by Ralph Stevenson measuring 10 1/2" in diameter. No manufacturers impress or printed back mark was used. The name of the view is printed on the front of the ware beneath the view. *Courtesy of the Collection of William R. & Teresa F. Kurau.*

New Orleans plate by Ralph Stevenson, 8" in diameter. *Courtesy of the Collection of William R. & Teresa F. Kurau.*

Thorps and Sprague, Albany plate by Ralph Stevenson, 8 1/4" in diameter. *Courtesy of the Collection of William R. & Teresa F. Kurau.*

Lace Border with Vases of Flowers

The center printed images here are scenes from Albany, New York. As with the Lace Border, the prints were produced in purple, pink, brown and black. The border includes vases of flowers along with the floral sprays over a lace background. The views are more limited, including the City Hall, Albany and Thorps and Sprague, Albany.

Hartford, State House

This view of the Connecticut state house was printed in a medium blue and was surrounded by a floral motif border depicting both flowers and leaves. The view was identified as State House, Hartford.

Vine Border

Printed back mark utilized by Ralph Stevenson for his Vine Border series with the name of the view printed in the mark. *Courtesy of the Collection of William R. & Teresa F. Kurau.*

United States architecture and the Battle of Bunker Hill are the subjects here. They were printed in a dark blue and sometimes had an embossed white rim. The border was composed of twining vines. The individual views included: the American Museum; Almshouse, Boston; Almshouse, New York; Battery, New York (Flagstaff Pavilion); Battle of Bunker Hill; Brooklyn Ferry; Capitol, Washington; City Hall, New York; Columbia College, New York; Deaf and Dumb Asylum, Hartford, Con.; Esplanade and Castle Garden, New York; Exchange, Charleston; Fort Gansevoort, New York; Fulton Market, New York; Hospital, Boston; Hospital, New York; Insane Asylum, New York; Lawrence Mansion, Boston; Masonic Hall, Philadelphia; Pennsylvania Hospital, Philadelphia; State House, Boston; and St. Patrick's Cathedral, Mott Street.

Battery, New York (Flagstaff Pavilion) plate by Ralph Stevenson measuring 7 1/4" in diameter. *Courtesy of the Collection of William R. & Teresa F. Kurau.*

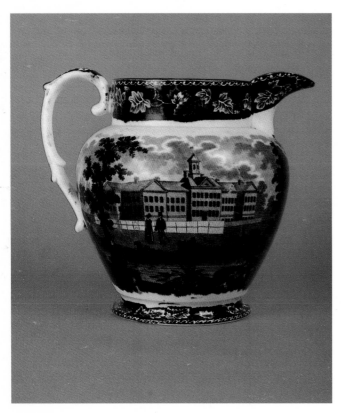

Almshouse, New York pitcher by Ralph Stevenson, 7 3/4" high. *Courtesy of the Collection of William R. & Teresa F. Kurau.*

Battery, New York (Flagstaff Pavilion) plate by Ralph Stevenson, 7" in diameter. *Courtesy of the Collection of William R. & Teresa F. Kurau.*

Battery, New York (Flagstaff Pavilion) plate by Ralph Stevenson, 7 3/8" in diameter. Note the white rim left around the rim in this print. *Courtesy of the Collection of William R. & Teresa F. Kurau.*

Battle Of Bunker Hill vegetable dish with a framed copy of the original art work. *Courtesy of the Collection of William R. & Teresa F. Kurau.*

A closer look at the **Battle Of Bunker Hill** vegetable dish by Ralph Stevenson. *Courtesy of the Collection of William R. & Teresa F. Kurau.*

Battle of Bunker Hill printed on the lid of a soup tureen by Ralph Stevenson. The view **Pennsylvania Hospital, Philadelphia** is printed on the outside. *Courtesy of the Collection of William R. & Teresa F. Kurau.*

Almshouse, Boston platter by Ralph Stevenson, 15" x 11". *Courtesy of the Collection of William R. & Teresa F. Kurau.*

Columbia College, New York plate by Ralph Stevenson, 8" in diameter. *Courtesy of the Collection of William R. & Teresa F. Kurau.*

Brooklyn Ferry platter by Ralph Stevenson, 11" x 8 1/2". This piece was once in the William Randolph Hearst collection. *Courtesy of the Collection of William R. & Teresa F. Kurau.*

Deaf & Dumb Asylum, Hartford pitcher by Ralph Stevenson, 9" high. *Courtesy of the Collection of William R. & Teresa F. Kurau.*

Columbia College, New York undertray with a **Fulton Market, New York** sauce tureen by Ralph Stevenson. A view of the **Masonic Hall, Philadelphia** is printed on the lid of the tureen. The undertray measures 9" x 6 1/4" and the tureen measures 5 1/4" high. *Courtesy of the Collection of William R. & Teresa F. Kurau.*

Esplanade And Castle Garden, New York platter by Ralph Stevenson, 17" x 13 1/4". *Courtesy of the Collection of William R. & Teresa F. Kurau.*

Fort Gansevoort, New York plate by Ralph Stevenson, 5 1/4" in diameter. *Courtesy of the Collection of William R. & Teresa F. Kurau.*

Exchange, Charleston vegetable dish and **Esplanade And Castle Gardens, New York** lid by Ralph Stevenson, 9 1/2" x 7 1/2". *Courtesy of the Collection of William R. & Teresa F. Kurau.*

Fulton Market, New York sauce tureen by Ralph Stevenson. A view of the **Masonic Hall, Philadelphia** is printed on the lid of the tureen and a print of **Columbia College, New York** is found on the undertray. The tureen measures 5 1/4" high and the undertray measures 9" x 6 1/4". *Courtesy of the Collection of William R. & Teresa F. Kurau.*

Hospital, Boston plate by Ralph Stevenson, 8 1/4" in diameter. *Courtesy of the Collection of William R. & Teresa F. Kurau.*

Lawrence Mansion, Boston (so called) large wash basin by Ralph Stevenson, 14 1/2" in diameter and 4 1/2" high. *Courtesy of the Collection of William R. & Teresa F. Kurau.*

Lawrence Mansion, Boston (so called) wash basin and pitcher set by Ralph Stevenson, 13 1/2" x 4" bowl and a 9" high pitcher. William R. Kurau points out that the scene actually features the "Boston Athenaeum" in the foreground with the spire of the "Octagon Church" behind it. *Courtesy of the Collection of William R. & Teresa F. Kurau.*

Pennsylvania Hospital, Philadelphia is printed on the side of this soup tureen, **Brooklyn Ferry** is printed inside the tureen and the **Battle of Bunker Hill** is printed on the lid. This piece was produced by Ralph Stevenson and measures 9" x 6 1/4". *Courtesy of the Collection of William R. & Teresa F. Kurau.*

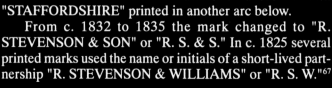

Washington and Lafayette

The center was a medallion bust of the generals, Washington and Lafayette printed in dark blue. The surrounding border was composed of flowers, scrolls and urns.

Marks

There is some confusion with these brother's marks. Both had the nasty habit of simply using the "STEVENSON" name as their mark, making it difficult to deduce which Stevenson, Andrew or Ralph, actually produced the ware. Ralph Stevenson did use an impressed "R. STEVENSON" mark or his initials as well. He also used an arced "STEVENSON" mark over a crown with "STAFFORDSHIRE" printed in another arc below.

From c. 1832 to 1835 the mark changed to "R. STEVENSON & SON" or "R. S. & S." In c. 1825 several printed marks used the name or initials of a short-lived partnership "R. STEVENSON & WILLIAMS" or "R. S. W."[67]

Impressed "STEVENSON" manufacturer's mark and printed "R. S." initials mark incorporated into the back mark following the name of the view. This "R. S." mark was used from c. 1810-1832. *Courtesy of the Collection of William R. & Teresa F. Kurau.*

Printed "R.S.W." manufacturer's mark used by Ralph Stevenson and Williams used in c. 1825 during the short-lived partnership of Stevenson and Aldborough Lloyd Williams. *Courtesy of the Collection of William R. & Teresa F. Kurau.*

Impressed "STEVENSON" manufacturer's mark which may be a source of confusion since both brothers Ralph and Andrew used this mark from c. 1816-1830. *Courtesy of the Collection of William R. & Teresa F. Kurau.*

Printed "R. STEVENSON & WILLIAMS COBRIDGE STAFFORDSHIRE" manufacturer's mark used in c. 1825. *Courtesy of the Collection of William R. & Teresa F. Kurau.*

The Stevenson Brothers and the Medallion Portraits

Andrew and Ralph Stevenson, and the partnership of Ralph Stevenson & Williams, produced Medallion Portraits with central images taken from views they were producing with other borders. Andrew Stevenson produced English views with his medallions enclosed with a rose border. Ralph Stevenson produced medallions with both his Floral, Scroll and Urn and his Vine borders. Ralph Stevenson and Williams produced medallions with the Acorn and Oak Leaves border.

Medallion portraits contained the images of Washington, Lafayette, Jefferson and Clinton English potters so frequently turned to when seeking American heroes to portray. One, two or four medallions could be used.

Small inset views of the Erie canal were also place in some of the borders. These views included:
the Aqueduct Bridge at Little Falls; the Aqueduct Bridge at Rochester; and the Entrance of the Erie Canal into the Hudson at Albany.

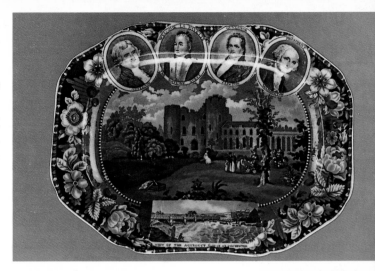

Tunbridge Castle, Surry central view with **View Of The Aqueduct At Rochester** by Andrew Stevenson, measuring 14 1/2" x 11". Several of the medallion series featured English central views. *Courtesy of the Collection of William R. & Teresa F. Kurau.*

Views Accompanying Four Portrait Medallions

These views include:
Albany Theatre, 1824; A View of the Late Protestant Dutch Church in the City of Albany...Erected in 1715...Pulled Down in 1806; Park Theatre, New York; Portrait Medallion Pitcher; Dulwich College, Essex; Dorney Court; Faulkbourn Hall; Niagara; Oatlands, Surrey; Summer Hall, Kent; Windsor Castle; and Writtle Lodge, Essex.

Park Theatre, New York plate by Ralph Stevenson & Williams, 10" in diameter. *Courtesy of the Collection of William R. & Teresa F. Kurau.*

Niagara plate by Andrew Stevenson measuring 10 1/4" in diameter and impressed with the circular "A. STEVENSON" crown mark. *Courtesy of the Collection of William R. & Teresa F. Kurau.*

Portrait Medallion Pitcher by Ralph Stevenson, 7" high. *Courtesy of the Collection of William R. & Teresa F. Kurau.*

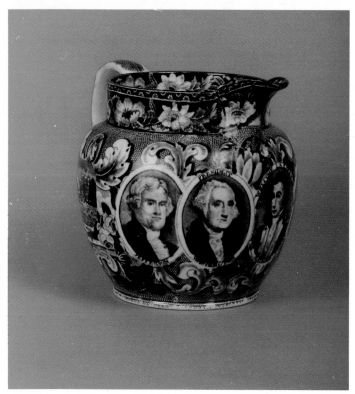

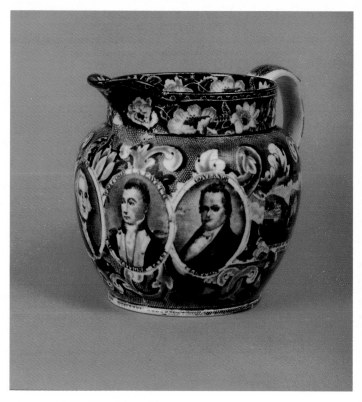

Portrait Medallion Pitcher with **Entrance Of The Canal Into The Hudson At Albany** and **View Of The Aqueduct Bridge At Rochester** Erie Canal views on either side by Ralph Stevenson, 5 1/4" high. *Courtesy of the Collection of William R. & Teresa F. Kurau.*

Views Accompanying Two Medallion Portraits

The views printed with two medallions included: the Capitol, Albany; Capitol, Washington; City Hotel, New York; Hospital, Boston; Park Theatre, New York; Boreham House, Essex; Faulkbourn Hall; and Remains of Covenhall.

Hospital, Boston plate by Ralph Stevenson with an **Entrance Of The Canal Into The Hudson At Albany** inset view, 8 1/4" in diameter. *Courtesy of the Collection of William R. & Teresa F. Kurau.*

Views Accompanying Single Medallion Portraits

These included views of the:
Battery, New York (Flagstaff Pavilion); Columbia College, New York; and St. Paul's Chapel, New York.

A Rare View

A rare printed view by Andrew Stevenson features the central image of the Charter Oak, Connecticut. The name in this print was accidentally reversed.

Joseph Stubbs

Joseph Stubbs produced earthenwares at Dale Hall, Longport, Burslem, Staffordshire from circa 1822-1835. Stubbs printed his wares in the dark blue popular early in America and did well in the export market. Briefly, from 1828 to 1830, Joseph Stubbs worked in partnership as Stubbs & Kent.[68]

Series and Views

Rose Border

Views surrounded by a border of roses in full bloom were limited to the City Hall, New York and the Boston State House.

Boston State House pitcher by Joseph Stubbs, 6 3/8" high. *Courtesy of the Collection of William R. & Teresa F. Kurau.*

City Hall, New York is printed on the other side of the pitcher by Joseph Stubbs, 6 3/8" high. *Courtesy of the Collection of William R. & Teresa F. Kurau.*

Connecticut Charter Oak plate impressed "STEVENSON" in an arc over a three masted sailing ship, attributed to Andrew Stevenson, and measuring 6 1/4" in diameter. With the reversed image, this is a rare piece indeed. *Courtesy of the Collection of William R. & Teresa F. Kurau.*

Spread Eagle Border

The printed back marks used with the Spread Eagle border. The name of the view is printed in the center of the mark. *Courtesy of the Collection of William R. & Teresa F. Kurau.*

Architectural and scenic views of the United States provide the central views. These were surrounded with borders featuring eagles with wings spread amidst an abundance of flowers and scrolls. The views included:
the Bank of the United States, Philadelphia; Church in the City of New York (Dr. Mason's); City Hall, New York; Fair Mount Near Philadelphia; Highlands, North River; Hoboken in New Jersey; Mendenhall Ferry; Nahant Hotel, Near Boston; New York Bay; Park Theatre, New York; State House, Boston; Upper Ferry Bridge Over the River Schuylkill; View at Hurl Gate, East River; and Woodlands, Near Philadelphia.

Church In The City Of New York (Dr. Mason's) plate by Joseph Stubbs, 6 1/4" in diameter. *Courtesy of the Collection of William R. & Teresa F. Kurau.*

Bank Of The United States, Philadelphia plate by Joseph Stubbs, 10" in diameter. *Courtesy of the Collection of William R. & Teresa F. Kurau.*

Fair Mount Near Philadelphia platter by Joseph Stubbs, 20 1/2" x 16 7/8". *Courtesy of the Collection of William R. & Teresa F. Kurau.*

Hoboken In New Jersey gravy boat with a **Upper Ferry Bridge Over The River Schuylkill** underplate by Joseph Stubbs. The gravy boat measures 4 1/4" high. The underplate measures 7 1/2" x 5 1/2". *Courtesy of the Collection of William R. & Teresa F. Kurau.*

Fair Mount Near Philadelphia plate by Joseph Stubbs, 6 3/4" in diameter. *Courtesy of the Collection of William R. & Teresa F. Kurau.*

Mendenhall Ferry platter by Joseph Stubbs, 16 1/2" x 13 1/2". The Mendenhall rope ferry was located just below the falls of the Schuylkill River in Pennsylvania. To the left is the Mendenhall Inn, opened early in the nineteenth century. It was a popular resort for Philadelphians hungry for a fine meal. *Courtesy of the Collection of William R. & Teresa F. Kurau.*

Park Theatre, New York plate by Joseph Stubbs, 6 1/4" in diameter. *Courtesy of the Collection of William R. & Teresa F. Kurau.*

Upper Ferry Bridge Over The River Schuylkill platter by Joseph Stubbs, 19" x 15 1/2". *Courtesy of the Collection of William R. & Teresa F. Kurau.*

State House, Boston platter by Joseph Stubbs measuring 12" x 14 1/2".
Courtesy of the Collection of William R. & Teresa F. Kurau.

Upper Ferry Bridge Over The River Schuylkill wash basin by Joseph Stubbs measuring 11 3/4" in diameter. *Courtesy of the Collection of William R. & Teresa F. Kurau.*

Upper Ferry Bridge Over The River Schuylkill plate by Joseph Stubbs, 8 1/4" in diameter. *Courtesy of the Collection of William R. & Teresa F. Kurau.*

Upper Ferry Bridge Over The River Schuylkill plate by Joseph Stubbs, 9" in diameter. *Courtesy of the Collection of William R. & Teresa F. Kurau.*

View Of New York Bay plate by Joseph Stubbs, 10" in diameter. This is a very rare piece. *Courtesy of the Collection of William R. & Teresa F. Kurau.*

Upper Ferry Bridge Over The River Schuylkill sauce tureen by Joseph Stubbs. *Courtesy of the Collection of William R. & Teresa F. Kurau.*

Woodlands, Near Philadelphia platter by Joseph Stubbs, 9 3/8" x 7 3/8". This is a rare piece. *Courtesy of the Collection of William R. & Teresa F. Kurau.*

Woodlands, Near Philadelphia plate by Joseph Stubbs, 6 5/8" in diameter. *Courtesy of the Collection of William R. & Teresa F. Kurau.*

Marks

During the years of production from c. 1822-1835 Joseph Stubbs used impressed marks reading either simply "STUBBS" or "JOSEPH STUBBS LONGPORT". The second was printed in a circular form. From c. 1828 to 1830, the circular impressed mark "STUBBS & KENT LONGPORT" was used.[69]

S. Tams & Company/Tams, Anderson & Tams

Little is known about the firms bearing the S. Tams & Company, Tams & Anderson or Tams, Anderson & Tams names. No records are currently known to exist for them. Under this name, however, transfer printed earthenwares were produced from circa 1820 to 1840 and exported to the American market.

Wares produced by these mysterious firms were limited in transfer printed decorations to two series of British views, a near copy of Robert Hamilton's Ruined Castle pattern and several American subjects.[70]

Series and Views

Several dark blue printed American views were produced including:
the Capitol at Harrisburg, PA; The Capitol, Washington; and United States Hotel, Philadelphia.

These were bordered with either foliage with a grotto center (the Capitol at Harrisburg) or flowers and leaves (both The Capitol and United States Hotel).

United States Hotel, Philadelphia plate by Tams, Anderson & Tams, 10" in diameter. *Courtesy of the Collection of William R. & Teresa F. Kurau.*

The Capitol, Washington bowl by Tams, Anderson & Company or Tams, Anderson & Tams, 10" in diameter and 3 1/2" high. This is a rare view. *Courtesy of the Collection of William R. & Teresa F. Kurau.*

Utica Tribute creamer, 5" high. *Courtesy of the Collection of William R. & Teresa F. Kurau.*

Utica Tribute plate measuring 7 3/4" in diameter. *Courtesy of the Collection of William R. & Teresa F. Kurau.*

Famous Naval Heroes

The central view is of a monument to the "Nautical Heroes of the War of 1812." It is printed in dark blue and features a floral border and an irregular central opening.

Famous Naval Heroes creamer measuring 4 3/4" high. The base of the monument reads "WASHINGTON, INDEPENDENCE, TRUXTUN". Thomas Truxtun commanded the Independence, and several other war ships, during the American Revolution with much success, capturing a number of vessels. An action of Truxtun's in 1781-1782 spurred George Washington to throw a dinner in his honor and declare Thomas Truxtun's services "worth a regiment." His naval service would extend into the nineteenth century. *Courtesy of the Collection of William R. & Teresa F. Kurau.*

Famous Naval Heroes creamer measuring 6 1/2" high. *Courtesy of the Collection of William R. & Teresa F. Kurau.*

Franklin Flying A Kite

If this single view is Benjamin Franklin flying the kite, it is in his early youth, long before his dabbling with electricity. The central view features a fairly primitive image of two boys, one flying a kite while the other rolls a hoop. A man with a tri-cornered hat and his arms folded over his chest looks on. These three are standing before a large church with a walled cemetery. The print was produced in a light blue and the border was a zig-zag design.

Great Fire, City of New York

Several views were produced of the New York City fire of December 16 and 17, 1835. Printed in light blue, green, purple, pink, brown and black, the various views were surrounded by a border of fire engines and eagles with their wings spread. While these are considered produced by an unknown manufacturer, it is possible that this design was produced by Thomas Dimmock. Dimmock used the single letter D as the distinguishing mark for his manufacturer's marks. This single letter appears in a variety of different printed marks. As with the mark used here, other marks by Dimmock also identify both the printed pattern and the body of the earthenware. In this mark and others, the body type is identified as Stone Ware.

Thomas Dimmock established himself in Shelton in c. 1828, producing earthenwares considered by the jury at the Great Exhibition of the Works of All Nations in London in 1851 to be of first-rate quality. His transfer printed patterns were admired for their neatness and good taste and for the general excellence of his wares. His firm remained in business until 1859.

Whether produced by Thomas Dimmock or not, the printed views of the conflagration included the Exchange, New York; Ruins, Merchant's Exchange; and Burning of Coenties Slip.

Harvard College

A view of Harvard College was produced in pink, brown or black surrounded by a border of roses held together by a single band.

Island of Saint Thomas

Views from around the island of Saint Thomas printed in black with a printed back mark including the name J. & M. Azevedo. This may be an importer. The views included: East View of the Town of Charlotte Amalie in the Island of St. Thomas; Southeast View of the Town of Charlotte Amalie in the Island of St. Thomas; Judge Bergs Residence; Mr. Kjaers Residence & Observatory; Southwest View of the Town of Charlotte Amalie in the Island of St. Thomas.

The printed back mark includes the name "J & M Azevedo", possibly the name of the importers of these wares. *Courtesy of the Collection of William R. & Teresa F. Kurau.*

East View Of The Town Of Charlotte Amalie In The Island Of St. Thomas platter, 11 1/8" x 10 1/4". *Courtesy of the Collection of William R. & Teresa F. Kurau.*

Left: Exchange, New York soup bowl measuring 10 1/4" in diameter. At the time of the fire, December 16, 1835, New York had been enjoying a robust trade with the Midwest via the Erie Canal. The effects of the fire were staggering, enveloping seven hundred buildings, fully sixteen million dollars worth of property. For a time, this brought the city to it's knees. Within days of the fire, three large lithographs of the event were produced by J. H. Bufford and published by the artist and J. Disturnell. These were quickly picked up in Staffordshire and put to earthenware. *Courtesy of the Collection of William R. & Teresa F. Kurau.*

Left: This D mark could be the manufacturer's mark of Thomas Dimmock. Dimmock was in business from c. 1828 to 1859. The name of the body of the ware "Stone Ware" and the name of the view are incorporated into the mark. *Courtesy of the Collection of William R. & Teresa F. Kurau.*

Southeast View Of The Town Of Charlotte Amalie In The Island Of St. Thomas platter, 12 3/4" x 10 1/4". *Courtesy of the Collection of William R. & Teresa F. Kurau.*

Judge Bergs Residence plate, 7" in diameter. *Courtesy of the Collection of William R. & Teresa F. Kurau.*

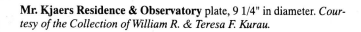

Mr. Kjaers Residence & Observatory plate, 9 1/4" in diameter. *Courtesy of the Collection of William R. & Teresa F. Kurau.*

Southwest View Of The Town Of Charlotte Amalie In The Island Of St. Thomas plate, 10 3/4" in diameter. *Courtesy of the Collection of William R. & Teresa F. Kurau.*

Lafayette Crowned At Yorktown

In this fanciful view, two angels crown General Lafayette with a heroes wreath. The print was produced in black and bordered either with black bands or copper luster. On hollow forms a second view, Surrender of Cornwallis, is presented.

Mount Vernon, The Seat of the Late Gen'l. Washington

Two patriotic reminiscence in print. The first depicts the general and his steed in front of Mount Vernon and the Potomac River. This image was printed in dark blue and surrounded by a border of large flowers.

The second is taken from the art work of William Birch, published in 1804. This is a tasteful three-quarters view of Mount Vernon and it's wooded surroundings. The title was printed across the top of the view. This image was printed in light blue or black on white porcelain wares. The border was composed of a simple dark blue cross-stitching.

Mount Vernon, The Seat Of The Late Gen'l. Washington teapot, 7" high. *Courtesy of the Collection of William R. & Teresa F. Kurau.*

Mount Vernon, Washington's Seat

Mount Vernon and the Potomac River, complete with sailing vessels, are presented in this view along with a small riding figure. Could this be George Washington himself? This depiction of Mount Vernon was also printed in dark blue with a border of large curling leaves and diminutive flowers.

Quebec

The city of Quebec is printed in dark blue in the background, the river and ship traffic appear in the foreground. The border consists of eagles and scrolls.

Quebec sugar bowl with an eagle and leaf border. The lid is missing. This is part of a tea set in this pattern. *Courtesy of the Collection of William R. & Teresa F. Kurau.*

Enoch Wood & Sons

The Wood family produced nearly as many potters as the Adams family, thankfully not unimaginatively named as a series of Williams. Of them, Enoch Wood did very well with finely crafted transfer printed wares. He was also among the first Staffordshire potters to develop the much-sought-after healthy export trade with the United States of America. In strengthening that trade, Enoch Wood produced approximately 58 American views, over 80 English views and a series of French views. All of these are collected in America today, continuing Wood's tie to the American market in a way he surely never dreamed possible.[72]

Enoch Wood & Sons produced their quality transfer printed earthenwares out of Burslem from 1818 to 1846. The early wares for export were produced in the deep cobalt blue best loved in America. The firm's capacity was tremendous. Records of a Philadelphia china broker in 1834 indicated that a single shipment from Wood & Sons totaled 262,000 pieces.[73]

Over time, Enoch Wood & Sons produced transfer prints which followed the popular trends of the day. Later prints were produced in colors other than blue and featuring romantic scenes in more open designs.

The most significant and appreciated of Enoch Wood & Son's output were (and are) the various series of views produced. Each piece in a dinner service was decorated with a different view. This would have turned a meal into an arm-chair tour of America many wished to take but, due to circumstances over which they had little control, could never have hoped to make themselves. A number of single view or pattern services were also produced.

Series and Views

Boston State House

This view depicts the Boston state house as it appeared from the Commons in 1804. It was printed in dark or medium blue surrounded by a border of blooming flowers.

Boston State House plate by Enoch Wood & Sons, 9 1/2" in diameter. *Courtesy of the Collection of William R. & Teresa F. Kurau.*

Boston State House saucer and **Boston Coffee Exchange** cup elegantly produced by Enoch Wood & Sons. *Courtesy of the Collection of William R. & Teresa F. Kurau.*

Celtic China

Printed back mark used on the Celtic China wares which includes the name of the view, the manufacturer's initials "E.W. & S." in use from c. 1818-1846 and the Celtic China name. *Courtesy of the Collection of William R. & Teresa F. Kurau.*

A combination of scenic views and views of a variety of American architecture decorate the centers of these prints. They were printed in light blue, green, purple, pink, brown and black and were encircled with a border of fruit and flowers. The views included:
Belleville on the Passaic River; Buffalo on Lake Erie; Castle Garden, Battery, New York; Columbus (Ga.); Fairmount Waterworks on the Schuylkill; Harvard College (two views); Highlands, Hudson River; Lake George; Natural Bridge, Virginia; New York from Staten Island; Niagara Falls; Pass in the Catskill Mountains; Riceborough, Georgia; Shipping Port on the Ohio, Kentucky; Transylvania University, Lexington, Kentucky; Trenton Falls; West Point, Military Academy; and Wooding Station on the Mississippi.

Castle Garden, Battery, New York large soup tureen by Enoch Wood & Sons, 14 1/2" wide, 10" high. Of this tureen Ellouise Larsen remarked that this was an extremely rare piece in brilliant proof condition. She also notes the view on the lid is unlisted and, at the time she was writing -- c. 1939, was unique. *Courtesy of the Collection of William R. & Teresa F. Kurau.*

Lake George, State Of New York well and tree platter by Enoch Wood & Sons measuring 19" x 14 3/4". *Courtesy of the Collection of William R. & Teresa F. Kurau.*

Trenton Falls plate by Enoch Wood & Sons measuring 7 3/4" in diameter. *Courtesy of the Collection of William R. & Teresa F. Kurau.*

Chancellor Livingston

The central view shows the steamboat named the Chancellor Livingston. It was printed in dark blue, bordered with large and small flowers with scrolls.

Chancellor Livingston sugar bowl by Enoch Wood & Sons, 5 1/2" high. *Courtesy of the Collection of William R. & Teresa F. Kurau.*

Eagle on Rock

An eagle prepares for flight from a rocky ledge as a steamboat sails by in the background. The print was produced in pink and purple with a floral border overlaying diamonds.

Eagle On Rock saucer by Enoch Wood & Sons measuring 6" in diameter. While the transfer is simplistic, this saucer is finely potted and is extremely thin in cross section. *Courtesy of the Collection of William R. & Teresa F. Kurau.*

Floral Border — Irregular or Grotto-shaped Center

A small series printed in dark blue featuring views of the Erie Canal, MacDonnough's Victory and Wadsworth Tower. The views were:
Commodore MacDonnough's Victory; Wadsworth Tower; Entrance of the Erie Canal into the Hudson at Albany; Erie Canal. Aqueduct Bridge at Rochester; and Erie Canal. View of the Aqueduct Bridge at Little Falls. The border consists of large blooming flowers with an irregular central opening.

Commodore MacDonnough's Victory sugar bowl by Enoch Wood & Sons, 6 3/4" high. *Courtesy of the Collection of William R. & Teresa F. Kurau.*

Commodore MacDonnough's Victory tea pot by
Enoch Wood & Sons, 8" high. *Courtesy of the Collection of William R. & Teresa F. Kurau.*

Commodore MacDonnough's Victory cup & saucer by Enoch Wood
& Sons. *Courtesy of the Collection of William R. & Teresa F. Kurau.*

Entrance Of The Erie Canal Into The Hudson At Albany plate by Enoch Wood & Sons, 10 1/2" in diameter. *Courtesy of the Collection of William R. & Teresa F. Kurau.*

Erie Canal. Aqueduct Bridge At Rochester cup plate by Enoch Wood & Sons, 4 3/4" in diameter. *Courtesy of the Collection of William R. & Teresa F. Kurau.*

Erie Canal. View of the Aqueduct Bridge At Little Falls soup bowl by Enoch Wood & Sons, 10 1/8" in diameter. *Courtesy of the Collection of William R. & Teresa F. Kurau.*

Entrance Of The Erie Canal Into The Hudson At Albany pitcher by Enoch Wood & Sons, 9 1/4" high. *Courtesy of the Collection of William R. & Teresa F. Kurau.*

Erie Canal. View of the Aqueduct Bridge At Little Falls cup plate by an unknown maker, 4 3/4" in diameter. Note the similarities in the central view and the unusual border. *Courtesy of the Collection of William R. & Teresa F. Kurau.*

Erie Canal. View of the Aqueduct Bridge At Little Falls pitcher by Enoch Wood & Sons. *Courtesy of the Collection of William R. & Teresa F. Kurau.*

Four Medallion — Floral Border Series

A variety of scenic views were presented in the center surrounded by four large medallions displaying urns and flowers around the border. These medallions were separated by blooming flowers. The prints were produced in light blue, purple, pink and brown. The views included: Castle Garden; Department of State, Washington; Dumb Asylum, Philadelphia; Harvard University; Monte Video; New Haven, State House; Northampden, Mass.; President's House, Washington; Race Bridge, Philadelphia; and Residence of S. Russell.

Franklin's Tomb

A dark blue print featuring Lafayette reclined in thought, gathering inspiration from the urn topped tomb marked Franklin. The border is floral. The print is entitled Lafayette at Franklin's Tomb.

Lafayette At Franklin's Tomb tea pot by Enoch Wood & Sons, 7 1/4" high. *Courtesy of the Collection of William R. & Teresa F. Kurau.*

Lafayette At Franklin's Tomb cup & saucer by Enoch Wood & Sons. *Courtesy of the Collection of William R. & Teresa F. Kurau.*

Lafayette At Franklin's Tomb coffee pot by Enoch Wood & Sons, 11" high. *Courtesy of the Collection of Lynn D. Trusdell.*

Lafayette At Franklin's Tomb sugar bowl by Enoch Wood & Sons, 5 1/4" high. *Courtesy of the Collection of William R. & Teresa F. Kurau.*

Lafayette At Franklin's Tomb tea pot by Enoch Wood & Sons, 7 3/4" high. *Courtesy of the Collection of William R. & Teresa F. Kurau.*

Lafayette At Franklin's Tomb creamer by Enoch Wood & Sons, 4 1/2" high. *Courtesy of the Collection of William R. & Teresa F. Kurau.*

The French Series

Also printed in dark blue, French prints include several views significant to Americans during this period which displayed Lafayette's family home, LaGrange. The borders were a combination of flowers, grapes and leaves. The views included:

Cascade de Gresy, Pres Chambery; Chapelle de Guillaume Tell; East View of LaGrange, the Residence of the Marquis Lafayette; Environs de Chambery; Hermitage en Dauphine; LaGrange the Residence of the Marquis Lafayette; Maison de Raphael; Moulin Pres de Royat, Dept du Puy de Dome; Moulin Sur La Marne a Charenton; Moulin Sur La Marne a Charenton; N.W. View of LaGrange, the Residence of the Marquis Lafayette; S.W. View of LaGrange, the Residence of the Marquis Lafayette; Vue D'une, Ancienne Abbey; Vue du Chateau de Coucy; Vue du Chateau Ermenonville; Vue de LaPorte Romaine a Andernach; Vue Prise en Savoie; Vue Prise Aux Environs de Francfort; Vue du Temple de Philosophie, Ermenonville; and several unnamed French views.

LaGrange The Residence Of The Marquis Lafayette soup bowl by Enoch Wood & Sons, 10 1/8" in diameter. Americans were interested in all aspects of General Lafayette's life including the appearance of his family home. *Courtesy of the Collection of William R. & Teresa F. Kurau.*

Lafayette At Franklin's Tomb pitcher by Enoch Wood & Sons, 8" high. *Courtesy of the Collection of William R. & Teresa F. Kurau.*

East View Of LaGrange, The Residence Of The Marquis Lafayette on a mahogany sewing box of the Federal period. These views were not limited to Staffordshire earthenwares in some cases. *Courtesy of the Collection of William R. & Teresa F. Kurau.*

Landing Of The Fathers At Plymouth, Dec. 22, 1620 plate by Enoch Wood & Sons, 10 1/4" in diameter. *Courtesy of the Collection of William R. & Teresa F. Kurau.*

General Jackson, Hero of New Orleans

This portrait bust of General Andrew Jackson relates to Jackson's victory over British troops in the War of 1812. That battle settled the question of ownership of the important port of New Orleans. The matter was actually settled shortly after the peace treaty was signed ending the war. Printed above the print was "General Jackson" and beneath was "Hero of New Orleans". The print was produced in red or black on a white plate with either a raised border with lustre paint or a single red line.

Landing of the Pilgrims

The central view depicted the Pilgrims landing at Plymouth Rock. These were printed in a dark or medium blue and surrounded by a border of eagles and scrolls. This view was entitled The Landing of the Fathers at Plymouth, Dec. 22, 1620.

Landing Of The Fathers At Plymouth, Dec. 22, 1620 pitcher by Enoch Wood & Sons. *Courtesy of the Collection of William R. & Teresa F. Kurau.*

Landing Of The Fathers At Plymouth, Dec. 22, 1620 cup plate by Enoch Wood & Sons, 3 5/8" in diameter. *Courtesy of the Collection of William R. & Teresa F. Kurau.*

Lafayette And Washington small plate by Enoch Wood & Sons measuring 5 1/2" in diameter. The blue feather edge was extremely popular in America in pearlware in the first quarter of the nineteenth century. *Courtesy of the Collection of William R. & Teresa F. Kurau.*

Lafayette and Washington

Twin medallion busts side-by-side display busts of Lafayette and Washington. Above the medallions is an eagle with wings spread and a ribbon clutched in it's claws. The ribbon contained the men's names. The print was produced in blue, pink, brown and black with a raised molded border, at times with a variety of colors applied.

Lafayette And Washington cup plate by Enoch Wood & Sons measuring 3 5/8" in diameter. Due to the small size of the cup plate only part of the central print was used. *Courtesy of the Collection of William R. & Teresa F. Kurau.*

Shell Border, Circular Center

Unlike the irregular or grotto-shaped shell border series, the circular centered shell border series provides a printed back mark with the name of the view. This variation of the Great Seal of America is the standard motif for the mark of this series. *Courtesy of the Collection of William R. & Teresa F. Kurau.*

These were dark blue printed American and Canadian views encircled by a shell border with a circular center framing the views. A trailing vine entwines along the edge of the circular center of the border. The views included: Belleville on the Passaic River; Castle Garden Battery, New York; Catskill House, Hudson; Catskill Mountains, Hudson River; City of Albany, State of New York; Fall of Montmorenci Near Quebec; Gilpin's Mills on the Brandywine Creek; Hudson River View; Highlands, Hudson River; Highlands at West Point, Hudson River; Highlands, Hudson River, Near Newburgh; Hope Mill, Catskill, State of New York; Lake George, State of New York; Marine Hospital, Louisville, Kentucky; Mount Vernon; New York Bay; Niagara Falls from the American Side; Passaic Falls, State of New Jersey; Pass in the Catskill Mountains; Pine Orchard House, Catskill Mountains; Quebec; Table Rock, Niagara; Tappan Bay from Greensburg; The Baltimore & Ohio Railroad (Incline); The Baltimore & Ohio Railroad (Level); The Capitol at Washington; Transylvania University, Lexington; View of Trenton Falls — Three people on the rocks; View of Trenton Falls — One man at the foot of the falls; West Point Military Academy; and White House, Washington.

Belleville On The Passaic River soup tureen with a **Hudson River View** ladle, a **New York Bay** print on the lid, and **Hope Mill, Catskill, State of New York** undertray by Enoch Wood & Sons. *Courtesy of the Collection of William R. & Teresa F. Kurau.*

Castle Garden Battery, New York by Enoch Wood & Sons measuring 18 1/2" x 14 1/4". *Courtesy of the Collection of William R. & Teresa F. Kurau.*

Two **Castle Garden Battery, New York** cup plates by Enoch Wood & Sons, 3 5/8" in diameter. *Courtesy of the Collection of William R. & Teresa F. Kurau.*

Catskill House, Hudson plate by Enoch Wood & Sons, 6 1/2" in diameter. *Courtesy of the Collection of William R. & Teresa F. Kurau.*

Falls Of Montmorenci Near Quebec plate by Enoch Wood & Sons, 9" in diameter. *Courtesy of the Collection of William R. & Teresa F. Kurau.*

City Of Albany, State of New York bowl by Enoch Wood & Sons measuring 9 1/8" in diameter. *Courtesy of the Collection of William R. & Teresa F. Kurau.*

Highlands, Hudson River, Near Newburgh by Enoch Wood & Sons measuring 6 1/2" in diameter. *Courtesy of the Collection of William R. & Teresa F. Kurau.*

Highlands, Hudson River small platter by Enoch Wood & Sons, 12 3/4" x 10 1/4". *Courtesy of the Collection of William R. & Teresa F. Kurau.*

Highlands At West Point, Hudson River plate by Enoch Wood & Sons measuring 6 1/2" in diameter. *Courtesy of the Collection of William R. & Teresa F. Kurau.*

Highlands, Hudson River small platter by Enoch Wood & Sons measuring 12 3/4" x 10". *Courtesy of the Collection of William R. & Teresa F. Kurau.*

Gilpin's Mills On The Brandywine Creek plate by Enoch Wood & Sons, 9 1/8" in diameter. *Courtesy of the Collection of William R. & Teresa F. Kurau.*

Mount Vernon, The Seat Of The Late Gen'l. George Washington by Enoch Wood & Sons, 6 1/2" in diameter. *Courtesy of the Collection of William R. & Teresa F. Kurau.*

Niagara Falls From The American Side platter by Enoch Wood & Sons, 14 3/4" x 11 1/2". *Courtesy of the Collection of William R. & Teresa F. Kurau.*

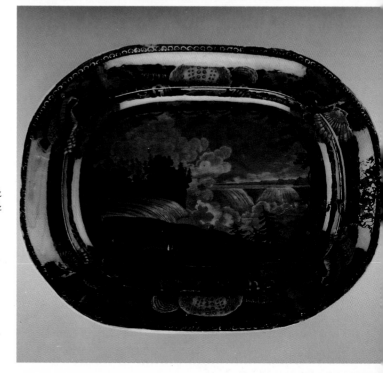

Pass In The Catskill Mountains plate by Enoch Wood & Sons measuring 10" in diameter. *Courtesy of the Collection of William R. & Teresa F. Kurau.*

Passaic Falls, State Of New Jersey sauce tureen, **Hudson River View** on the lid and ladle, and **Pass In The Catskill Mountains** undertray by Enoch Wood & Sons. The tureen measures 6 1/2" high, the undertray measures 8" x 6 1/4" and the ladle measures 8" in length. *Courtesy of the Collection of William R. & Teresa F. Kurau.*

Pine Orchard House, Catskill Mountains plate by Enoch Wood & Sons, 9 3/4" in diameter. This is a very fine and clear print. *Courtesy of the Collection of William R. & Teresa F. Kurau.*

Quebec square bowl by Enoch Wood & Sons, 9 1/2" square and 2" high. *Courtesy of the Collection of William R. & Teresa F. Kurau.*

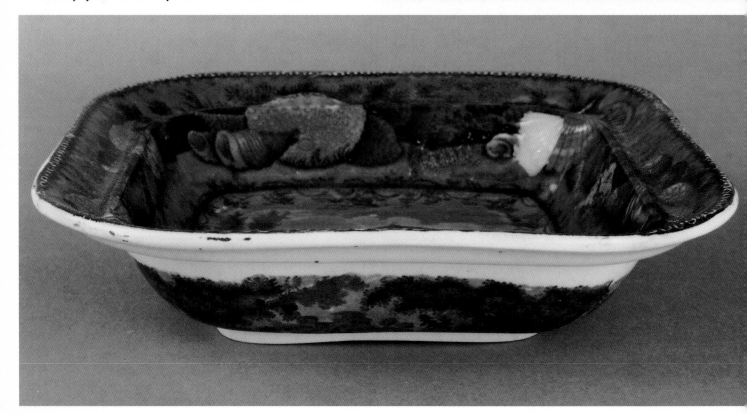

Tappan Bay From Greenburgh platter by Enoch Wood & Sons, 18 1/2" x 14 1/2". *Courtesy of the Collection of William R. & Teresa F. Kurau.*

Table Rock, Niagara soup bowl by Enoch Wood & Sons, 10 1/4" in diameter. *Courtesy of the Collection of William R. & Teresa F. Kurau.*

The Baltimore & Ohio Railroad (Incline) plate by Enoch Wood & Sons, 9" in diameter. With the tiny English engine depicted riding the level grade, a more powerful stationary engine, depicted here, would be necessary to handle even gentle inclines. *Courtesy of the Collection of William R. & Teresa F. Kurau.*

The Baltimore & Ohio Railroad (Level) plate by Enoch Wood & Sons, 10" in diameter. This tiny engine in the print was developed by George Stephenson in 1825 and was never used in America. R. T. Haines Halsey suggests this print was produced to commemorate the laying of the first rail of the Baltimore & Ohio Railroad on July 4, 1828 and was produced prior to the event or at that time. This would explain the presence of an engine that never ran American rails. *Courtesy of the Collection of William R. & Teresa F. Kurau.*

The Capitol, Washington plate by Enoch Wood & Sons, 6 1/2" in diameter. *Courtesy of the Collection of William R. & Teresa F. Kurau.*

View Of Trenton Falls (three people on the rocks to the left) plate by Enoch Wood & Sons, 7 3/4" in diameter. *Courtesy of the Collection of William R. & Teresa F. Kurau.*

View Of Trenton Falls (one person at the foot of the falls) plate by Enoch Wood & Sons, 6 1/2" in diameter. *Courtesy of Lynn D. Trusdell.*

White House, Washington plate by Enoch Wood & Sons measuring 5 3/4" in diameter. *Courtesy of the Collection of William R. & Teresa F. Kurau.*

West Point Military Academy platter by Enoch Wood & Sons. 12" x 9 1/2". *Courtesy of the Collection of William R. & Teresa F. Kurau.*

Shell Border, Irregular or Grotto-shaped Center

This was a series of predominantly nautical views with both American and foreign subjects printed in dark cobalt blue. The borders were comprised of clusters of shells with an irregular inner opening creating a central grotto appearance. The shells complement the nautical themes and also reflect the growing nineteenth century fascination with the natural world. The views included:
Cadmus (so-called); Cape Coast Castle on the Gold Coast, Africa; Chief Justice Marshall, Troy (a side-wheel steam ship); Chiswick on the Thames; Christianburg, Danish Settlement on the Gold Coast, Africa; Commodore MacDonnough's Victory; Constitution and the Guerriere (so-called); Cowes Harbor; Dartmouth; Dix Cove on the Gold Coast, Africa; East Cowes, Isle of Wight; Erith on the Thames; Marine Hospital, Louisville, Kentucky; Near Calcutta; Ship of the Line in the Downs; Southampton, Hampshire; The Beach at Brighton; The Eddistone Lighthouse; The Kent, East Indiaman; Union Line; View of Dublin; View of Liverpool; Wadsworth Tower; Whitby; Yarmouth, Isle of Wight; Ship, Anchored; Ship, Under Half Sail; Two Sailboats and Rowboat; and Two Sailboats.

Christianburg, Danish Settlement On The Gold Coast, Africa well and tree platter by Enoch Wood & Sons, 18 1/2" x 14 1/2". *Courtesy of the Collection of William R. & Teresa F. Kurau.*

Christianburg, Danish Settlement On The Gold Coast, Africa platter by Enoch Wood & Sons, 18 1/2" x 14 1/2". The American flag flying from the closest ship piques interest in this view among American collectors. *Courtesy of the Collection of William R. & Teresa F. Kurau.*

Cape Coast Castle On The Gold Coast, Africa platter by Enoch Wood & Sons measuring 18 1/2" x 14 1/2". Rather than being featured in a printed back mark, the name of the view is usually presented within the view itself. *Courtesy of the Collection of William R. & Teresa F. Kurau.*

Dix Cove On The Gold Coast, Africa soup tureen by Enoch Wood & Sons, 10 1/2" high. *Courtesy of the Collection of William R. & Teresa F. Kurau.*

Commodore MacDonnough's Victory plate by Enoch Wood & Sons, 10" in diameter. *Courtesy of the Collection of William R. & Teresa F. Kurau.*

Constitution And The Guerriere (so called) plate by Enoch Wood & Sons, 10 1/4" in diameter. Cannon's blazed and the Stars and Stripes snapped as the 44-gun frigate Constitution battered the British frigate Guerière off the Maine coast in this transfer. This was another American triumph of the War of 1812. Today the restored Constitution holds a place of honor in the United States Navy as the oldest ship in the fleet. *Courtesy of the Collection of William R. & Teresa F. Kurau.*

Marine Hospital, Louisville, Kentucky plate by Enoch Wood & Sons, 9" in diameter. *Courtesy of the Collection of William R. & Teresa F. Kurau.*

A Ship Of The Line In The Downs vegetable dish by Enoch Wood & Sons, 9 3/4" square and 5 3/4" high. *Courtesy of the Collection of William R. & Teresa F. Kurau.*

Wadsworth Tower creamer by Enoch Wood & Sons, 4 1/2" high. *Courtesy of the Collection of William R. & Teresa F. Kurau.*

Southampton, Hampshire plate by Enoch Wood & Sons, 7 1/2" in diameter. *Courtesy of the Collection of William R. & Teresa F. Kurau.*

Wadsworth Tower coffee pot by Enoch Wood & Sons, 10 1/4" high.
Courtesy of the Collection of William R. & Teresa F. Kurau.

Two Sailboats cup plate by Enoch Wood & Sons, 4 3/4" in diameter. *Courtesy of the Collection of William R. & Teresa F. Kurau.*

Wadsworth Tower sugar bowl by Enoch Wood & Sons, 6 3/4" high. *Courtesy of the Collection of William R. & Teresa F. Kurau.*

Trefoil Border

Three small, pleasant and unrelated views printed in dark view surrounded by a trefoil border separated by knobs. The views included the:
Cadmus; Castle Garden, Battery, New York; and a Cottage in the Woods.

Cadmus (so called) cup plate by Enoch Wood & Sons, 3 5/8" in diameter. *Courtesy of the Collection of William R. & Teresa F. Kurau.*

Cadmus (so called) cup plate by Enoch Wood & Sons, 3 5/8" in diameter. This is a clearer print. *Courtesy of the Collection of William R. & Teresa F. Kurau.*

Washington

The central view depicts either a statue of Washington produced by Canova or a vase on a stand. It was printed in light blue, green, brown and black, or a combination of these. The border was a combination of scenic medallions, shells and seaweed.

Washington's Tomb

Lafayette again regarding an urn capped tomb, this time marked Washington. Again the floral border and dark blue ink were used. The print was entitled Lafayette at Washington's Tomb.

Castle Garden, Battery, New York cup plate by Enoch Wood & Sons, 3 5/8" in diameter. *Courtesy of the Collection of William R. & Teresa F. Kurau.*

Lafayette At Washington's Tomb large platter by Enoch Wood & Sons measuring 19" x 15". This platter once belonged to R.T. Haines Halsey and was pictured in his 1899 book. *Courtesy of the Collection of William R. & Teresa F. Kurau.*

Washington Standing at His Tomb, Scroll in Hand

In a rather bizarre dark blue print epitomizing a nineteenth century view of death as romantic in a melancholy sort of way, Washington regards his own tomb. A scroll dangles from his hand. The tomb is an urn marked Washington. Ethereal light cascades down from the left. Ships pass on the waters behind him. Again, a floral border surrounds the scene. The print was titled Washington Standing at His Tomb, Scroll in Hand.

Washington Standing At His Tomb, Scroll in Hand sugar bowl by Enoch Wood & Sons, 6 3/4" high. *Courtesy of the Collection of William R. & Teresa F. Kurau.*

Washington Standing At His Tomb, Scroll in Hand creamer by Enoch Wood & Sons, 4 3/4" high. *Courtesy of the Collection of William R. & Teresa F. Kurau.*

Washington Standing At His Tomb, Scroll in Hand tea pot by Enoch Wood & Sons, 7 1/2" high. An odd tea service, allowing the participants to take their tea with the shade of the departed president. *Courtesy of the Collection of William R. & Teresa F. Kurau.*

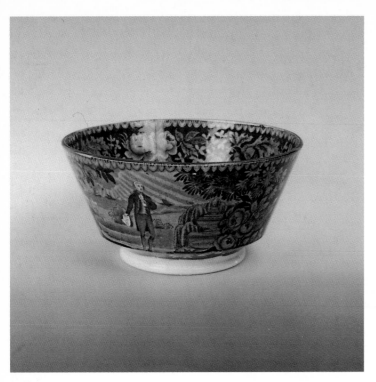

Washington Standing At His Tomb, Scroll in Hand waste bowl by Enoch Wood & Sons, 6 3/4" in diameter and 3 1/4" high. *Courtesy of the Collection of William R. & Teresa F. Kurau.*

Marks

Enoch Wood & Sons used a variety of impressed marks featuring the full name or the initials of the firm. The location of the pottery was also used either as "BURSLEM" or "BURSLEM STAFFORDSHIRE". Two marks include the American eagle emblem with wings spread, shield on chest and arrows and olive branch in claws. The mark "E. & E. WOOD" was used briefly in c. 1840 and referred to Enoch and Edward Wood.[74]

The impressed "WOOD" manufacturer's mark is the least helpful identifying mark. It was first used by Enoch Wood in c. 1784 and continued to be used throughout the life of the Enoch Wood & Sons firm from 1818-1846. *Courtesy of the Collection of William R. & Teresa F. Kurau.*

Impressed circular manufacturer's mark reading "ENOCH WOOD & SONS BURSLEM WARRANTED SEMI CHINA" used from 1818-1846 for finely printed wares made for export to the American market. *Courtesy of the Collection of William R. & Teresa F. Kurau.*

A closer and clearer view of the circular impressed manufacturer's mark above in use from 1818-1846. *Courtesy of Lynn D. Trusdell.*

Conclusion

Historical Staffordshire wares had a dual role in the early to mid-nineteenth century. For the British pottery industry, these wares were good-will ambassadors, reestablishing good trade relations with a now independent nation. For the Americans, historical Staffordshire bolstered the national pride. The prints reminded Americans of past glories, of heroes come and gone, and provided a grand tour of important places most would never see for themselves.

For collectors today, historical Staffordshire prints of American patriots and views provide a glimpse into the dreams and aspirations of the free people of a young nation proud of it's recent past and present accomplishments. It provides a view of the United States as Americans wanted it to be then ... and wish it had been today.

United States Hotel, Philadelphia plate by Tams, Anderson & Tams measuring 10 1/4" in diameter. Historical Staffordshire provided a view of the United States as Americans wanted it to be for them then ... and that we wish it had been today. *Courtesy of the Collection of William R. & Teresa F. Kurau.*

Bibliography

Adams, William Hampton & Sarah Jane Boling. "Status and Ceramics for Planters and Slaves on Three Georgia Coastal Plantations." *Historical Archaeology* 23 (1), 1989.

Albertson, Karla Klein. "Tableware in Transition. Collecting Historical Staffordshire." *Early American Life* 20, 1989.

Arman, David & Linda. *Historical Staffordshire. An Illustrated Check-List.* Danville, Virginia: Arman Enterprises, Inc., 1974.

The Art Journal Illustrated Catalogue. *The Industry of All Nations 1851.* London: George Virtue, 1851.

Cameron, Elisabeth. *Encyclopedia of Pottery & Porcelain. 1800-1960.* New York: Facts on File Publications, 1986.

Chevalier, Michael. *Society, Manners & Politics in the United States Being a Series of Letters on North America.* Boston, Massachusetts: Weeks, Jordan & Company, 1839.

Coysh, A. W. *Blue and White Transfer Ware, 1780-1840.* London & Vancouver: David & Charles, 1970.

Coysh, A. W. & R. K. Henrywood. *The Dictionary of Blue and White Printed Pottery. 1780-1880.* Volume I. Woodbridge, Suffolk: Antique Collectors' Club, 1982.

Dean, Patricia. *The Official Identification Guide to Pottery & Porcelain.* Orlando, Florida: The House of Collectibles, Inc., 1984.

Deetz, James. *In Small Things Forgotten.* Garden City, New York: Anchor Press/Doubleday, 1977.

Dickens, Charles. *Pictures from Italy and American Notes.* Bloomsbury: The Nonesuch Press, 1938. [reprint of 1842 original]

Godden, Geoffrey A. *Encyclopaedia of British Pottery and Porcelain Marks.* New York: Bonanza Books, 1964.

_____, *The Concise Guide to British Pottery and Porcelain.* London: Barrie & Jenkins, 1990.

Halsey, R. T. Haines. *Pictures of Early New York on Dark Blue Staffordshire Pottery.* New York: Dover Publications, Inc., 1974.[reprint of 1899 original]

Hughes, Bernard & Therle. *The Collector's Encyclopaedia of English Ceramics.* London: Abbey Library, 1968.

Hirsch, E. D., Jr., Joseph F. Kett & James Trefil. *The Dictionary of Cultural Literacy. What Every American Needs to Know.* Second Edition. Boston, Massachusetts: Houghton Mifflin Company, 1993.

Jewitt, Llewellynn. *The Ceramic Art of Great Britain.* Poole, Dorset, England: New Orchard Editions Ltd., 1985. [reprint of 1877 original]

Kurau, William R. & Teresa. *Historical Staffordshire and Collector's Items.* Lampeter, PA: personal printing (catalogues), 1993-1994.

Laidacker, Sam. *Anglo-American China, Part I.* Bristol, Pennsylvania: Sam Laidacker, 1954. Second Edition.

Larkin, Jack. *The Reshaping of Everyday Life. 1790-1840.* New York: Harper & Row, Publishers, 1988.

Larson, Ellouise B. *American Historical Views on Staffordshire China.* New York, 1939; reprinted and revised 1950, 1975.

Little, W. L. *Staffordshire Blue. Underglaze Blue Transfer-printed Earthenware.* New York: Crown Publishers, Inc., 1969.

Lockett, T. A. & P. A. Halfpenny (ed.). *Creamware & Pearlware. The Fifth Exhibition from the Northern Ceramic Society.* Stoke-on-Trent: George Street Press Ltd., 1986.

McCutcheon, Marc. *The Writer's Guide to Everyday Life in the 1800s.* Cincinnati, Ohio: Writer's Digest Books, 1993.

Miller, George L. "Classification and Economic Scaling of Nineteenth Century Ceramics." *Historical Archaeology* 14(2), 1980.

_____, "A Revised Set of CC Index Values for Classification and Economic Scaling of English Ceramics from 1787 to 1880." *Historical Archaeology* 25(1), 1991.

Newhouse, Elizabeth L. *Inventors and Discoverers. Changing Our World.* Washington, D.C.: National Geographic Society, 1988.

Noël Hume, Ivor. *All the Best Rubbish.* New York: Harper & Row, Publishers, 1974.

_____, *A Guide to Artifacts of Colonial America.* New York: Alfred A. Knopf, 1985.

Panati, Charles. *Panati's Extraordinary Endings of Practically Everything and Everybody.* New York: Harper & Row, Publishers, 1989.

Royal Commission. *Reports by the Juries on the Subject in the Thirty Classes into Which the Exhibition was Divided.* Volume III. London: W. Clowes & Sons, Printers, 1852.

Scott, John Anthony. *The Story of America.* Washington, D.C.: National Geographic Society, 1984.

Seidel, John L. "'China Glaze' Wares on Sites from the American Revolution: Pearlware Before Wedgwood?" *Historical Archaeology* 24(1), 1990.

Smiles, Samuel. *Josiah Wedgwood F.R.S. His Personal History.* Ann Arbor, Michigan: Plutarch Press, 1971. [reprint of 1894 edition]

Smillie, James. *Green-Wood Illustrated.* New York: R. Martin, 1847.

Snyder, Jeffrey B. *Flow Blue. A Collector's Guide to Pattern, History, and Values.* West Chester, Pennsylvania: Schiffer Publishing Ltd., 1992.

_____, *Historic Flow Blue.* Atglen, Pennsylvania: Schiffer Publishing Ltd., 1994.

Endnotes

Introduction

1. Ivor Noël Hume. *All the Best Rubbish* (New York: Harper & Row, Publishers, 1974), 147.
2. Llewellynn Jewitt. *The Ceramic Art of Great Britain* (Poole, Dorset, England: New Orchards Editions Ltd., 1985) [reprint of 1877 original], 381; Jeffrey B. Snyder. *Historic Flow Blue* (Atglen, PA: Schiffer Publishing, 1994), 41.

Chapter One

1. Jeffrey B. Snyder. *Flow Blue. A Collector's Guide to Pattern, History, and Values* (West Chester, PA: Schiffer Publishing, 1992), 8-9.
2. ibid, 9; Ivor Noël Hume, A Guide to Artifacts of Colonial America (New York: Alfred A. Knopf, 1985), 128-131; John L. Sidel. "'China Glaze' Wares on Sites from the American Revolution: Pearlware Before Wedgwood?" *Historical Archaeology* 24(1): 1990, 82.
3. William Hampton Adams & Sarah Jane Boling. "Status and Ceramics for Planters and Slaves on Three Georgia Coastal Plantations." *Historical Archaeology* 23(1): 1989, 75.
4. Sidel, "'China Glaze' Wares on Sites from the American Revolution: Pearlware Before Wedgwood?", 84.
5. ibid, 88-90; T.A. Lockett & P.A. Halfpenny (ed.), Creamware & Pearlware. (Stoke-on-Trent, England: George Street Press Ltd., 1986), 46.
6. Snyder, *Flow Blue.*, 9-10.
7. ibid, 10.
8. ibid, 10.
9. ibid, 10.
10. ibid, 11.
11. George L. Miller. "A Revised Set of CC Index Values for Classification and Economic Scaling of English Ceramics from 1787 to 1880." *Historical Archaeology* 25(1): 1991, 9.
12. Miller, "A Revised Set of CC Index Values for Classification and Economic Scaling of English Ceramics from 1787 to 1880.", 9; Miller, "Classification & Economic Scaling of Nineteenth Century Ceramics."; R.T. Haines Halsey. *Pictures of Early New York on Dark Blue Staffordshire Pottery* (New York: Dover Publications, Inc., 1974 [reprint of 1899 original], 14.
13. Miller, "A Revised Set of CC Index Values for Classification and Economic Scaling of English Ceramics from 1787 to 1880.", 9.
14. Hume, *All The Best Rubbish*, 147; Sidel, "'China Glaze' Wares on Sites from the American Revolution: Pearlware Before Wedgwood?", 93.
15. Hume, *All The Best Rubbish*, 147; Samuel Smiles. *Josiah Wedgwood F.R.S. His Personal History* (Ann Arbor, MI: Plutarch Press, 1971), 59.
16. Hume, *All The Best Rubbish*, 155.

Chapter Two

1. Snyder, *Historic Flow Blue*, 9.
2. Karla Klein Albertson, "Tableware in Transition. Collecting Historical Staffordshire." *Early American Life* 20, 1989, 41-44; Snyder, *Flow Blue*, 11.

3. E.D. Hirsch, Jr., Joseph F. Kett & James Trefil. *The Dictionary of Cultural Literacy* (Boston, MA: Houghton Mifflin Company, 1993), 259, 266-267.
4. ibid, 245; Albertson, "Tableware in Transition. Collecting Historical Staffordshire.", 66.
5. Snyder, *Historic Flow Blue*, 10-11.
6. ibid, 37.
7. ibid, 38.
8. Jack Larkin, *The Reshaping of Everyday Life. 1790-1840* (New York: Harper & Row, Publishers, 1988), 158; Charles Dickens, *Pictures From Italy and American Notes* (Bloomsbury, England: The Nonesuch Press 1938 [reprint]), 83.
9. Snyder, *Historic Flow Blue*, 11.
10. Dickens, *Pictures From Italy and American Notes*, 24, 95.
11. ibid, 115, 122.
12. ibid, 27.
13. Larkin, *The Reshaping of Everyday Life. 1790-1840*, 275-276.
14. ibid, 276.
15. ibid, 300.
16. Charles Panati, *Panati's Extraordinary Endings of Practically Everything and Everybody* (New York: Harper & Row, Publishers, 1989), 28-29; James Smillie, *Green-Wood Illustrated* (New York: R. Martin, 1847), 1.
17. Panati, *Panati's Extraordinary Endings of Practically Everything and Everybody*, 26.
18. ibid, 29.
19. Hume, *All the Best Rubbish*, 46-48.
20. Halsey. *Pictures of Early New York on Dark Blue Staffordshire Pottery*, 41-43.
21. ibid, 41-43; Larkin, *The Reshaping of Everyday Life. 1790-1840*, 297; Hume, *All the Best Rubbish*, 46-48.
22. John Anthony Scott, *The Story of America* (Washington, D.C.: National Geographic Society, 1984), 122.
23. Elizabeth L. Newhouse, Inventors and Discoverers. Changing Our World (Washington, D.C.: National Geographic Society, 1988), 36.
24. Dickens, *Pictures From Italy and American Notes*, 1.
25. Scott, *The Story of America*, 126.
26. ibid, 126.
27. ibid, 122.
28. Halsey, *Pictures of Early New York on Dark Blue Staffordshire Pottery*, 263.
29. Chevalier, Michael, Society, Manners & Politics in the United States Being a Series of Letters on North America (Boston, MA: Weeks, Jordan & Company, 1839), 82.
30. Snyder, *Historic Flow Blue*, 12.
31. ibid, 12.
32. James Deetz, In Small Things Forgotten (Garden City, New York: Anchor Press/Doubleday, 1977), 60.
33. Snyder, *Historic Flow Blue*, 14-17.
34. Larkin, *The Reshaping of Everyday Life. 1790-1840*, 174; Geoffrey C. Ward, Ric Burns & Ken Burns, The Civil War. An Illustrated History (New York: Alfred A. Knopf, Inc., 1990), 123.
35. Larkin, *The Reshaping of Everyday Life. 1790-1840*, 144-145.
36. ibid, 160-161; Geoffrey A. Godden, *The Concise*

Guide to British Pottery and Porcelain (London: Barrie & Jenkins, 1990), 187.

Chapter Three

1. A.W. Coysh & R.K. Henrywood, *The Dictionary of Blue and White Printed Pottery. 1780-1880* (Woodbridge, Suffolk: Antique Collectors' Club, 1982), 10-11; Elisabeth Cameron, *Encyclopedia of Pottery & Porcelain. 1800-1960* (New York: Facts on File Publications, 1986), 331.
2. Coysh & Henrywood, *The Dictionary of Blue and White Printed Pottery. 1780-1880*, 9-10.
3. ibid, 10-11.
4. Geoffrey A. Godden, *British Porcelain. An Illustrated Guide* (New York: Clarkson N. Potter, Inc./ Publisher, 1974), 228-230.
5. ibid, 228-230.
6. ibid, 228-230.
7. Coysh & Henrywood, *The Dictionary of Blue and White Printed Pottery. 1780-1880*, 8.
8. Garth Clark, *Ceramic Art: Comment & Review 1882-1977* (New York: Dutton, 1978), 84.
9. Godden, *British Porcelain. An Illustrated Guide*, 228-230.
10. Snyder, *Flow Blue*, 16.
11. Godden, *British Porcelain. An Illustrated Guide*, 228-230; Bernard & Therle Hughes, *The Collector's Encyclopaedia of English Ceramics* (London: Abbey Library, 1968), 36.
12. ibid, 228-230; W.L. Little, *Staffordshire Blue Underglaze Blue Transfer-printed Earthenware* (New York: Crown Publishers, Inc., 1969), 10.
13. Hume, *All The Best Rubbish*, 154.

Chapter Four

1. Miller, "A Revised Set of CC Index Values for Classification and Economic Scaling of English Ceramics from 1787 to 1880.", 9.
2. ibid, 9.
3. Hughes, *The Collector's Encyclopaedia of English Ceramics*, 151.
4. Miller, "A Revised Set of CC Index Values for Classification and Economic Scaling of English Ceramics from 1787 to 1880.", 9.
5. Coysh & Henrywood, *The Dictionary of Blue and White Printed Pottery. 1780-1880*, 8-9.
6. ibid, 9.
7. ibid, 10.
8. Halsey, *Pictures of Early New York on Dark Blue Staffordshire Pottery*, 14; Coysh & Henrywood, *The Dictionary of Blue and White Printed Pottery. 1780-1880*, 10.
9. Coysh & Henrywood, *The Dictionary of Blue and White Printed Pottery. 1780-1880*, 10.
10. ibid, 10-11.
11. ibid, 10-11; Russel Blaine Nye, Society & Culture in America, 1830-1860 (New York: Harper Torchbooks, Harper & Row Publishers, 1974), 159, 172-173.
12. Coysh & Henrywood, *The Dictionary of Blue and White Printed Pottery. 1780-1880*, 11.
13. Snyder, *Flow Blue*, 26-27.

14. Godden, *British Porcelain. An Illustrated Guide*, 26.
15. ibid, 26.
16. ibid, 26.
17. ibid, 27.
18. ibid, 29.
19. ibid, 29.

Chapter Five

Used throughout this section for reference to pattern names and manufacturers' marks were David & Linda Arman, *Historical Staffordshire. An Illustrated Check-List* (Danville, VA: Arman Enterprises, Inc., 1974), Sam Laidacker, *Anglo-American China* (Bristol, PA: Sam Laidacker, 1954), and Geoffrey A. Godden, *Encyclopaedia of British Pottery and Porcelain Marks* (New York: Bonanza Books, 1964).

1. Jewitt, *The Ceramic Art of Great Britain*, 423; Coysh & Henrywood, *The Dictionary of Blue and White Printed Pottery. 1780-1880*, 16; Hughes, *The Collector's Encyclopaedia of English Ceramics*, 10-11.
2. Hughes, *The Collector's Encyclopaedia of English Ceramics*, 10-11; Godden, *The Concise Guide to British Pottery and Porcelain*, 22.
3. Jewitt, *The Ceramic Art of Great Britain*, 563-564.
4. ibid, 563-564.
5. Godden, *Encyclopaedia of British Pottery and Porcelain Marks*, 21-22.
6. Coysh & Henrywood, *The Dictionary of Blue and White Printed Pottery. 1780-1880*, 87.
7. Hughes, *The Collector's Encyclopaedia of English Ceramics*.
8. Arman, *Historical Staffordshire. An Illustrated Check-List*, 9.
9. Godden, *Encyclopaedia of British Pottery and Porcelain Marks*, 151-152.
10. Godden, *The Concise Guide to British Pottery and Porcelain*, 74; A.W. Coysh, *Blue and White Transfer Ware, 1780-1840* (London & Vancouver: David & Charles, 1970), 26.
11. Godden, *The Concise Guide to British Pottery and Porcelain*, 74.
12. Snyder, *Flow Blue*, 11.
13. Jewitt, *The Ceramic Art of Great Britain*, 468.
14. ibid, 469.
15. ibid, 469.
16. Coysh & Henrywood, *The Dictionary of Blue and White Printed Pottery. 1780-1880*, 125.
17. Jewitt, *The Ceramic Art of Great Britain*, 457; Godden, *Encyclopaedia of British Pottery and Porcelain Marks*, 231.
18. Coysh, *Blue and White Transfer Ware, 1780-1840*, 207.
19. Godden, *Encyclopaedia of British Pottery and Porcelain Marks*, 255-256.
20. Coysh, *Blue and White Transfer Ware, 1780-1840*, 38; Coysh & Henrywood, *The Dictionary of Blue and White Printed Pottery. 1780-1880*, 156, 158.
21. Godden, *Encyclopaedia of British Pottery and Porcelain Marks*, 278.
22. Coysh & Henrywood, *The Dictionary of Blue and White Printed Pottery. 1780-1880*, 163.
23. Godden, *Encyclopaedia of British Pottery and Porcelain Marks*, 289.
24. Coysh & Henrywood, *The Dictionary of Blue and White Printed Pottery. 1780-1880*, 169.
25. Godden, *Encyclopaedia of British Pottery and Porcelain Marks*, 303.
26. Coysh & Henrywood, *The Dictionary of Blue and White Printed Pottery. 1780-1880*, 169.
27. Godden, *Encyclopaedia of British Pottery and Porcelain Marks*, 305-306.
28. Coysh & Henrywood, *The Dictionary of Blue and White Printed Pottery. 1780-1880*, 173.
29. Godden, *Encyclopaedia of British Pottery and Porcelain Marks*, 318-319.
30. Coysh, *Blue and White Transfer Ware, 1780-1840*, 102, 108, 127; Coysh & Henrywood, *The Dictionary of Blue and White Printed Pottery. 1780-1880*, 173.
31. Godden, *Encyclopaedia of British Pottery and Porcelain Marks*, 321.
32. Coysh & Henrywood, *The Dictionary of Blue and White Printed Pottery. 1780-1880*, 197.
33. Godden, *Encyclopaedia of British Pottery and Porcelain Marks*, 349.
34. Coysh & Henrywood, *The Dictionary of Blue and White Printed Pottery. 1780-1880*, 242; Godden, *The Concise Guide to British Pottery and Porcelain*, 424; Royal Commission, *Reports by the Juries on the Subject of the Thirty Classes into Which the Exhibition was Divided* (London: W. Clowes & Sons, Printers, 1852), 1190.
35. Godden, *Encyclopaedia of British Pottery and Porcelain Marks*, 423.
36. Godden, *The Concise Guide to British Pottery and Porcelain*, 125; Jewitt, *The Ceramic Art of Great Britain*, 488.
37. Cameron, *Encyclopedia of Pottery & Porcelain. 1800-1960*, 220; Jewitt, *The Ceramic Art of Great Britain*, 488.
38. The Art Journal Illustrated Catalogue, *The Industry of All Nations, 1851* (London: George Virtue, 1851), 240.
39. Godden, *Encyclopaedia of British Pottery and Porcelain Marks*, 428-430; Hughes, *The Collector's Encyclopaedia of English Ceramics*.
40. ibid, 428.
41. ibid, 429.
42. Coysh & Henrywood, *The Dictionary of Blue and White Printed Pottery. 1780-1880*, 244.
43. Godden, *Encyclopaedia of British Pottery and Porcelain Marks*, 432.
44. Coysh & Henrywood, *The Dictionary of Blue and White Printed Pottery. 1780-1880*, 252-253.
45. Godden, *Encyclopaedia of British Pottery and Porcelain Marks*, 449.
46. Coysh & Henrywood, *The Dictionary of Blue and White Printed Pottery. 1780-1880*, 282.
47. Godden, *Encyclopaedia of British Pottery and Porcelain Marks*, 491.
48. Cameron, *Encyclopedia of Pottery & Porcelain. 1800-1960*, 263; Coysh & Henrywood, *The Dictionary of Blue and White Printed Pottery. 1780-1880*, 286.
49. Jewitt, *The Ceramic Art of Great Britain*, 565.
50. Godden, *Encyclopaedia of British Pottery and Porcelain Marks*, 501.
51. Godden, *The Concise Guide to British Pottery and Porcelain*, 152-153; Hughes, *The Collector's Encyclopaedia of English Ceramics*, 128; Royal Commission, *Reports by the Juries on the Subject of the Thirty Classes into Which the Exhibition was Divided*, 1189-1190.
52. Coysh & Henrywood, *The Dictionary of Blue and White Printed Pottery. 1780-1880*, 302.
53. Hughes, *The Collector's Encyclopaedia of English Ceramics*, 128; Godden, *The Concise Guide to British Pottery and Porcelain*, 152-153.
54. Jewitt, *The Ceramic Art of Great Britain*, 493.
55. Godden, *Encyclopaedia of British Pottery and Porcelain Marks*, 533-534; Hughes, *The Collector's Encyclopaedia of English Ceramics*, 128.
56. Coysh, *Blue and White Transfer Ware, 1780-1840*, 60; Coysh & Henrywood, *The Dictionary of Blue and White Printed Pottery. 1780-1880*, 306.
57. Godden, *Encyclopaedia of British Pottery and Porcelain Marks*, 548.
58. Coysh & Henrywood, *The Dictionary of Blue and White Printed Pottery. 1780-1880*, 332; E.D. Hirsch, Jr., et al., The Dictionary of Cultural Literacy. (Boston, MA: Houghton Mifflin Co., 1993), 260.
59. Godden, *Encyclopaedia of British Pottery and Porcelain Marks*, 571.
60. Coysh, *Blue and White Transfer Ware, 1780-1840*, 86; Coysh & Henrywood, *The Dictionary of Blue and White Printed Pottery. 1780-1880*, 349.
61. ibid, 86; ibid, 349.
62. Godden, *Encyclopaedia of British Pottery and Porcelain Marks*, 596.
63. Coysh & Henrywood, *The Dictionary of Blue and White Printed Pottery. 1780-1880*, 349-350; Hughes, *The Collector's Encyclopaedia of English Ceramics*, 140-141.
64. ibid, 349-350; ibid, 140-141.
65. ibid, 349-350; ibid, 140-141.
66. ibid, 349-350; ibid, 140-141.
67. Godden, *Encyclopaedia of British Pottery and Porcelain Marks*, 596-597.
68. Coysh, *Blue and White Transfer Ware, 1780-1840*, 88; Coysh & Henrywood, *The Dictionary of Blue and White Printed Pottery. 1780-1880*, 352.
69. Coysh & Henrywood, *The Dictionary of Blue and White Printed Pottery. 1780-1880*, 352; Godden, *Encyclopaedia of British Pottery and Porcelain Marks*, 601.
70. Coysh & Henrywood, *The Dictionary of Blue and White Printed Pottery. 1780-1880*, 356.
71. Coysh & Henrywood, *The Dictionary of Blue and White Printed Pottery. 1780-1880*, 356; Godden, *Encyclopaedia of British Pottery and Porcelain Marks*, 733.
72. Coysh, *Blue and White Transfer Ware, 1780-1840*, 94; Hughes, *The Collector's Encyclopaedia of English Ceramics*, 159; Godden, *The Concise Guide to British Pottery and Porcelain*, 195.
73. Coysh & Henrywood, *The Dictionary of Blue and White Printed Pottery. 1780-1880*, 408.
74. ibid, 408; Godden, *Encyclopaedia of British Pottery and Porcelain Marks*, 685-686.

Price Guide

Values vary immensely according to the condition of the piece, the location of the market, and the overall quality of the design and manufacture. Condition is always of paramount importance in assigning a value. Prices in the Midwest differ from those in the West or East, and those at specialty antique shows will vary from those at general shows. And, of course, being at the right place at the right time can make all the difference.

All these factors make it impossible to create an absolutely accurate price list, but we can offer a guide. The prices reflect what one could realistically expect to pay at retail or auction.

The left hand number is the page number. The letters following it indicate the position of the photograph on the page: T=top, L=left, R=right, TL=top left, TR=top right, C=center, CL=center left, CR=center right, B=bottom, BL=bottom left, BR=bottom right. Sequential numbers following immediately after these letters indicate the position of the piece in a series of pieces reading from left to right or top to bottom. The right hand column of numbers are the estimated price ranges in United States dollars.

page	position	dollar value						
5	CL	over 3500	26	TR1	450-550		BL	over 2000
	CR	375-475		TR2	150-200	47	TL	over 3000
6	TL	over 3000		BR	800-1200		CR	800-1200
	B1	4000-5000	27	TL	400-500		BL	800-1200
	B2	1000-1500		CL	300-350		BR	over 1200
	B3	2000-3000		C	250-300	48	TL	over 1500
7	TL	2000-3000		CR	over 1500		TR	275-375
	CL	700-900		BL	2000-2500		BL	over 3000
	BR	450-500	28	TR	2000-2400		BR	900-1200
10	T1	1500		B	3000-3500	49	TL/C	900-1200
	T2	2500	29	CR	over 3500		BL/BR	over 1000
	T3	1000-1500		BL	over 1800	50	TL/TR	over 1000
11	CL	350-450	31	B	450-550		CL	750-900
12	BL	over 2500	33	BR	over 2000		CR	over 1000
13	TL	over 500	34	TL	300		BR	over 3000
	BL	250-325		TR	250-300	51	TR	over 1500
14	T	1500		CL	over 400		CR	over 900
	CL	1000	35	TR	350		BL	250-300
	BR	over 12000		CR	over 1500	52	TL	275-350
15	BL	over 4000	36	CL	90-125		TR/CR	75-125
16	CR	over 2500	40	TL	900-1200		BR	75-125
17	TL	1500 cup plate		TR	500-700	53	TL	1200
	CL	over 1500		CL	125-175		TR	225-325
	CR	over 1000		BR	300-350		CL	over 200
	BR	900-1100	41	TL	75-150		CR	75-125
18	TL	375-475		TR	500-900		BR	75-125
	TR	1000-1500	42	TL/CL	1000-1500	54	TL	over 1500
19	TL	550-650	43	TL	over 2000		TR	125-175
	CL	2500-3500		TR	1000-1500		BL	over 1500
	CR	over 2000		CL	250-300		BR	over 275
20	CR	125-175		CR/BR	over 3000	55	TL	over 1500
	BL	375-475	44	TL	900-1400		CR	175-225
21	TR	150-200		CL/BR	600-800		BL	350-450
	CL	1800-2200		CR	350-450	56	CR	375-475
	BR	900-1200	45	TL	250-350	57	TR	125-150
22	CL	1500-2500		TR	2500-3000		BL	125-150
23	TR	850		BL	over 2000	58	CL	150-175
	CL	175		BR	250-300		BR	75-125
	BR	over 1000	46	TL	over 2000		TR/CR	over 1800
24	BR	125		TR	350-450	59	B	over 1800
25	CL	750		CL	375-475	60	CL	125
	CR	800-900		CR	450-500		CR	over 900

No.	Pos	Price
61	TR	475-575
	CR	475-575
	BL	450-550
62	TL	250-350
	CL	over 900
	BR	500-600
63	TL	125-150
	TR/BR	150-175
	CL	125-175
64	TL	350
	TR	175-200
	CL	450-600
	CR	350-450
65	TR	over 3000
	CR	over 3000
	BR	over 4000
66	TL	600-800
	CL/BR	600-750
	CR	600-750
67	TL	over 14000
	TR	600-800
	CL/BR	over 5000
68	CR/BR	350-425
69	TL	325-375
	CL	75-110
70	CL	500-600
71	CL	125
	CR	175 cup only
73	TL	275-375
	CL	175-275
	CR	150-200
	BR	175-275
74	TL	275-375
	CL	110-140
	BR	110-140
75	TR	700-900
	CR	200-275
	BL	over 2500
76	TL	over 800
	CL	over 1500
	CR	over 1500
	BR	900-1200
77	TL	900-1200
	CR	350-450
	BL	900-1200
78	TR	375-475
	BL/CR	700-900
79	TL	325-375
	TR	250-300
	BR1	450-600
	BR2	150-200
81	TL	700-900
	CL/BR	over 2000
	CR	over 2000
82	TR	450-600
83	TR	over 1500
	CL	1000-1250
84	TR	over 2500
	CL	over 1400
	CR	over 2500
85	TL	over 3000
87	TL	275-350
	CL	over 1000
	BR	325-375
88	TL	900-1200
	TR	800-1100
	CL	900-1200
	CR	475-575
89	TR	300-350
	CL	125-150
	CR	275-300
90	TR	500-650
	BL	over 900
	BR	500-650
91	TL	500-650
	TR	over 3000
	BL	over 3000
	BR	over 5000
92	TL	1200-1500
	TR	450-600
	CL	over 2500
	CR	over 900
	BL	2500
93	TL	over 2400
	CL	1000-1200
	CR/BR	1800-2400
94	TL	2500
	TR	300-350
	CL	1300-1500
	BR	3000-3500
95	TL	over 5000
	CR	over 5000
96	TR	over 6000
	CR	over 2500
	BL	over 2500
97		over 12000
98		over 12000
99	CL	over 2500
	CR1	700-900
	CR2	700-900
100	TR	800
	BL	475-575
101	TL	over 1500
	CL	250-325
	BR	1200-1500
102	TL	over 600
	TR	over 1200
	B	900-1200
103	TL	over 900
	TR	250-325
	B	250-325
104	TR	over 1000
	B	over 1200
105	TR	over 900
	B	275-325
106	TR	900-1200
	BL/CR	over 1500
107	TR/BR	400 cup only
108		250-300 plate
109	TR	275-350
	B	375-475
110	TR	475-575
	CL	475-575
	BR	over 1200
111	TL	over 1200
	CR	over 1200
	BL	500-600
115	CL	over 1000
116	CL	225-275
	BL	over 800
	BR	over 2500
117	TR	1000-1200
118	TL	over 800
	BL	100-125
	BR	750-900
119	T	950-1250
120	B	450-550
	TL	800-950
	TR	750-850
	BL	1200-1500
	BR	800-950
121	TR	over 2000
	BL	1200-1500
122	TR	over 1500
	B	350-375
123	TR	over 1200
	B	over 1400
124	TL	800-900
	BL	1200
	CR	250-350
125	TR	200-225
	CR/BR	over 1200
126	TL	375-475
	TR	600-900
	B	600-900
127	B	7000-9000
128	TL	over 1500
	BL/BR	300-350
129	TL	350-650
	TR	250-350
	B	550-650
130	TL	800-900
	B	over 1800
131	TR	800-900
	B	over 1800
132	TR	475-575
	CR	800-1100
	BR	over 1500
133	TL	450-650
	CR/B	over 3500
134	TL	550-650
	CR/B	over 1500
135	TL	over 1500
	B	450-550
136	TL	700-900
	C	700-900
137	TL	550-650
	B	350-400
138	TL	350-400
	TR	over 1000
	B	over 1500
139	TR	over 2000
	C	over 2000
	BL	over 1500
140		4000-4500
141	T	375-475
	B	900-1250
142		375-475
143		over 2000
144	T	700-900
	B	250-350
145		over 1700
146	TL	350-400
	B	600-750
147	TR	300-350
	B	300-350
148	TL	300-350
149	TR	900-1200
	CL	800-900
	B	950-1400
150	T	500-600
151	B	900-1200

Index